RENTING and LETTING

a Consumer Publication

Consumers' Association
publishers of **Which?**
14 Buckingham Street
London WC2 6DS

a Consumer Publication

edited by   Edith Rudinger

published by   Consumers' Association
publishers of **Which?**

© Consumers' Association March 1985
revised edition January 1987

ISBN 0 340 39964 5
     0 85202 339 1

photoset by Paston Press, Loddon, Norfolk
printed in Great Britain

RENTING AND LETTING

contents

This book describes the legal implications
of renting or letting a home
in the private or public sector
in England and Wales.
It does not apply in Scotland
and Northern Ireland.

introduction

The law relating to landlord and tenant is complicated and the process of new legislation goes on and on. At the time of going to press with this book in December 1986, the Housing and Planning Act 1986 has just received its royal assent. It will affect the council tenant's right to buy and has other provisions with respect to public sector housing. As with all new legislation, how it will work in practice has yet to be seen, but we can indicate in some relevant sections of the book what has been proposed.

Other proposals which have yet to be formulated in detail were contained in the Queen's speech in November 1986: to strengthen the rights of people living in private blocks of flats, and improve the management and repairs of mansion blocks. The planned legislation would also give tenants more right to information about their service charges, and tighter control over the money they pay.

Over the past 60-odd years, successive governments have added layers of new laws, rules and regulations in an attempt to protect tenants, and control landlords' income from land, and promote the supply of housing.

At the beginning of the twentieth century, the majority of lettings were by private landlords for investment purposes. By and large, tenants were free to remain in their rented homes undisturbed for as long as they liked, with little or no alteration in the rent. After the first world war, the demand for housing was greater than the supply, and rents soared. A landlord could easily rid himself of a tenant who could not afford to pay a higher rent, by serving a simple notice to quit, and then letting to a new tenant at that higher rent. Parliament introduced the Increase of Rent and Mortgage Interest (War Restrictions) Act 1915, preventing landlords who owned homes within specified rateable values from increasing the rent, and limiting their right to recover possession. Although the 1915 Act was intended to be a temporary measure, provisions to control rents and give tenants security of tenure have regulated lettings in the private sector ever since (apart from a short period of decontrol in the 1950's). In 1980 this security was extended to council tenants.

Today, the principal Acts governing the private sector include:

○ the *Rent Act 1977* as amended by the *Housing Act 1980* and the *Rent (Amendment) Act 1985* under which most lettings by private landlords fall;

○ the *Landlord and Tenant Act 1985* imposing compulsory repair obligations on landlords of short lettings (that is, for less than 7 years);

○ the *Landlord and Tenant Act 1954* encompassing long leases at low rents, leases of premises with mixed residential and business use and lettings by an approved body;

○ the *Leasehold Reform Act 1967* which gives tenants of houses held under a long lease at a low rent the right to call for an extended lease or the freehold;

○ The *Housing Act 1985* which regulates the rights of council tenants;

○ The *Protection from Eviction Act 1977* which affords basic protection against harassment and unlawful eviction to residential occupiers, in both the private and public sector.

Not all sections of the various Acts of Parliament are relevant to the ordinary residential tenant or licensee, or to his landlord. We have picked out those that do apply and put them together under headings that may be of importance if there is a dispute.

The statutes alone are not all – it is the way the courts have interpreted them that matters. Inevitably, the situations that end up in court are not open-and-shut and only the more complicated ones go on to the appeal court or, in the last resort, to the House of Lords. Where appropriate, we have put in references to decided cases because they indicate the way the courts are thinking and are likely to decide future cases.

This book does not deal in detail with the situation when all goes well. Rather, it tries to anticipate how things might go wrong and what to do to avoid this, and highlights the areas of dispute where the law can give guidance. The first step for enforcing the law either as landlord or as tenant is to know how it applies to various situations. Human nature, housing shortage, the need for the landlord to make some profit from his property, and the tenant to have a decent place to live, are the background to many of the disputes that arise.

Throughout this book

for 'he' read 'he or she'

leases and licences

English law recognises two forms of legal ownership of land only, freehold and leasehold. Freehold is the closest we can get to absolute or total ownership of property (in legal theory all land belongs to the Crown and freeholders are 'tenants-in-chief' of the Crown who pay no rent). A freehold can last for ever (and will only end if the current freeholder dies, leaving no relatives to inherit without having made a will). By contrast, leasehold ownership lasts for a definite period and the leaseholder pays a periodic sum of money, rent, to the landlord in return for the right to occupy and enjoy the property. The length of his entitlement to occupation depends (in theory, at least) on what he has agreed with the landlord.

Because leasehold ownership lacks the potential for everlastingness, it is often regarded as inferior to freehold ownership. But in economic terms a person granted a long lease or a short lease with security of tenure (security of tenure means that the leaseholder has the right to stay on in the property after the end of the lease), has an asset every bit as valuable as a freehold.

The terms 'lease' and 'tenancy' tend to be used interchangeably and do not have separate technical meanings; the word 'lease' is also used to describe the document or deed under which the leaseholder's right to occupy and enjoy the property is granted. The leaseholder is sometimes called the 'lessee' but more often the 'tenant'. The person or organisation granting the lease may be described as the 'lessor' or 'landlord'. At the end of the tenancy the landlord will be entitled to the property freed from the tenant's rights, except where the law provides otherwise. The landlord is said to own the 'reversion' in the property because ultimately the property will revert to him. His interest during the lifetime of the lease is called 'the reversion'. A validly created lease remains binding on any subsequent purchaser of the reversion (that is, a new landlord).

The landlord need not necessarily be the freeholder. He may have only a leasehold interest himself, but can create out of his own lease a sub-lease to another person, called a sub-lessee or subtenant. There may be many such interests in one property. The freeholder is the head-landlord. The parties between him and the actual occupier will be both tenants under the lease they hold and landlords under the lease they grant. They are sometimes called 'intermediate' or 'mesne' landlords. Each sub-lease must be for a period that is at least one day shorter than the lease out of which it was granted.

As well as specifying the rent payable and the length of the lease, most agreements between landlord and tenant contain many other terms setting out the rights and duties of the parties, for example, as to the carrying out of repairs, the tenant's use of the property, and so on. In addition, the law implies certain terms into some tenancy agreements, which impose obligations on the parties, usually the landlord. Such terms are collectively referred to as 'covenants'. If they are written into the lease, they are called 'express covenants', if implied by law, 'implied covenants'. Express and implied covenants are discussed later on in the book.

In many ways, a lease resembles a contract for the hire of goods, the tenant hiring property instead of, for example, a car. However, the law treats hiring property differently to hiring a car.

A person who hires a car can drive it where and when he pleases, but he gets no rights of ownership over the car. A lease confers on the tenant an interest in the land. He can sell ('assign') this interest, mortgage it, leave it by will, grant a sub-lease and so on. In other words, he has much the same powers of dealing with the land (that is, the property) as the freeholder has, except that the tenant's powers cease to exist when the lease ends.

Granting a lease is not the only way in which a landowner (freeholder or tenant) can profit from letting someone live in his vacant property. He can merely permit someone to stay there, so that his being on the property is not a trespass, unlawful entry or squatting. It can be agreed that the permission should last for a certain length of time and a sum similar to rent may be charged for the occupation. The permission may be on other express terms – about provision of furniture, breakages, damage, cleaning and the like. Such an arrangement, if genuine, is known as a licence. A guest staying at a hotel is a licensee, and so are lodgers and theatregoers.

licence

A licence is a personal arrangement between the licensor and the licensee. It usually forms part of a contract and can therefore be terminated only in accordance with the terms of the contract. A licensee has no proprietary interest (that is, he has no stake in the property) and his licence cannot usually bind a third party: if a new landlord buys the premises, he has the right to evict the licensee from it, even if he knew of the arrangement at the time of buying. All that the licensee can do is to sue the original licensor for damages, that is monetary compensation for breach of contract. But the courts have, on occasions, decided that a residential licence was irrevocable and capable of binding a new owner, where to do otherwise would have caused gross injustice (for example where the residential licensee was an old lady or someone seriously ill).

More importantly, most of the statutory provisions which confer considerable protection on tenants do not apply to licensees. From the landlord's point of view, controlled rents and sitting tenants can reduce the capital value of property by up to two-thirds of its vacant possession value. Landlords (and their legal advisers) have there- fore sought to employ the licence as a means of avoiding being caught by the legislation. At one time, the courts were sympathetic towards landlords granting residential licences instead of leases, provided that both parties understood the nature of the transaction they were entering into. But in 1985 the House of Lords, the most senior court, upset the applecart for residential landlords and effectively put paid to this particular method of Rent Act avoidance. As a by-product, many former licensees were turned into would-be tenants, protected by the Rent Act.

In a case of dispute, a person who occupies as his home property belonging to another will obviously be keen to establish that he has a lease rather than a licence. A landlord may wish to establish the opposite.

It is, therefore, in the interests of anyone who has been, or is in the process of, renting or letting to look closely at the lease/licence distinction, and in particular at those arrangements which will continue to create licences.

characteristics of a lease, and how a licence differs from it

For a tenancy to exist at law it must satisfy three requirements:

○ it must be for a definite period of time (a tenancy is, after all, a slice in time in the use of someone else's property)
○ exclusive possession must be granted
○ it must be created in the proper manner (this is discussed in the next section of the book).

for a definite period
The length (minimum or maximum) of the lease must be certain. A definite period can mean:

(i) a single period ending on a specified date, for example after 99 years. This is a fixed term lease/tenancy.

In a fixed term lease, the maximum duration of the term must be known. It does not matter that the lease contains provisions which mean that it may be ended prematurely. For example, at the beginning of the second world war it became common to grant leases 'for the duration of the war', but it was established that such a grant was void because no one knew when the war would end. Temporary legislation was introduced to convert these grants into ten-year leases (so that the maximum duration was known) terminable by one month's notice by either party at the end of the war. This device can be used in any case where it is desired that a lease should end on the happening of an uncertain event. For example, if a tenant is waiting for his newly-built house to be finished, he can be granted a fixed term lease of his present accommodation (for, say, two years) terminable by one month's notice when his new house is ready.

In fact, most fixed term leases contain provisions for premature termination. It would be rare to find a fixed term lease which does not allow the landlord to bring the lease to an end if, for example, the tenant does not pay the rent.

(ii) a short but definite period in the first place (a month, a week, a year) which will continue for further periods of that length until ended by notice to quit. This is known as a <u>periodic lease/ tenancy</u>.

In a periodic tenancy, the minimum duration is always known: a month, a year, a week or whatever period the tenancy was initially granted for. The maximum duration of a periodic tenancy can never be known until one party serves a notice to quit.

exclusive possession
Without exclusive possession there can be no lease, only a licence. The grant must give the occupier the right to use the premises as his home, to the exclusion of all others, including the landlord. Most tenancy agreements have a clause giving (in legal terms 'reserving') to the landlord the right to come in and inspect the condition of the premises and possibly to carry out repairs (and even where no such right is expressly reserved, the law may imply it). This does not detract from the occupier's exclusive possession. On the contrary, it reinforces it: in a true tenancy the landlord commits trespass if he enters the premises without the tenant's permission. On the other hand, where the landlord retains control of the premises, as is usual in the case of a hotel, for example, there can only be a licence.

is it a lease or a licence?

At one time, exclusive possession was the decisive factor in determining whether a lease or a licence had been created. If the occupier had exclusive possession he was a tenant; if he did not, he must be regarded as a mere licensee. However, it rapidly became apparent that this was too simplistic an approach, because there are a number

of specific situations where an occupier does have exclusive possession of premises and yet is not, in law, regarded as a tenant. For
instance, a buyer who goes into possession of the property after
exchange of contracts but before completion, and an employee who
is allowed to live in his employer's premises for the better performance of his work, are both licensees. More of a problem were
the 'generosity cases': family or friends who were provided with
living accommodation as an act of kindness and who then wanted to
outstay their welcome. Out of these cases grew the notion that
although exclusive possession was an important factor, the real test
was the intention of the parties. If it was intended to give the
occupier a stake in the premises rather than a personal privilege to
stay there, then he was a tenant. If not, he was a licensee.

the intention of the parties?

Once the intention of the parties became the crucial factor, it did not
take the courts long to realise that they had laid a minefield.
Landlords who were in the business of providing residential accommodation started to draft and give their occupiers 'licence agreements' which purported to negative the intention to grant a tenancy:
terms were purposefully short, parties were described as 'licensor'
and 'licensee', a 'licence fee' was payable, occupiers were required
to sign statements recognising that they had no protection under the
Rent Act, and so on. But these agreements did not always achieve
their intended purpose of creating a licence rather than a lease
because the courts were prepared to go behind the label the parties
had used and look at the substance of the agreement.

The climax came in 1978 when the courts gave the go-ahead to the
use of 'non-exclusive licence' as a legitimate means of Rent Act
avoidance. Couched in licence language in order to negative any
intention to create a tenancy, this device also purported to deny the
other essential characteristic of a tenancy, exclusive possession, by
including a term entitling the licensor to insist that he, or a third
party of his choice, should be allowed to share the premises. In the
case of *Somma v. Hazlehurst, 1978*, an unmarried couple were
granted two separate agreements by Mrs Somma to occupy one
bed-sittingroom. The effect of these agreements was to ensure that

the room was neither let to one partner nor to both, and that Mrs Somma could install other occupiers from time to time. Although this was patently an illusory right, the Court of Appeal saw no objection to the arrangement and concluded that a licence had been created, not a lease. They saw no objection in law or on grounds of public policy to a landlord (or a landlady) arranging his affairs in such a way as to bring himself outside the operation of the Rent Act.

This moral neutrality did not last long: 1985 saw a return to the traditional method of distinguishing between a lease and a licence. In the case of *Street v. Mountford, 1985*, the House of Lords made it clear that where, in return for a money payment, an occupier is granted exclusive possession of residential premises, for a term, there is a strong presumption that he is a tenant.

There are now only two situations in which the occupier will not be regarded as a tenant. First, where he can be regarded as within one of the special categories mentioned earlier, for example a purchaser let into possession of property under a contract for sale. And second, where the circumstances show that there was no intention to enter into legal relations at all (that is, enter into a legally binding contract). This second category covers cases where exclusive occupation of accommodation is given out of friendship or generosity. But it will not cover those arrangements which are deliberately worded so as to negative an intention to create a tenancy. (In *Street v. Mountford*, Mrs Mountford had signed this declaration: "I understand and accept that a licence in the above form does not and is not intended to give me a tenancy protected under the Rent Act".) In other words if, in law, the end result is a tenancy, it is irrelevant that the parties intended to create a licence only.

The 'licence agreement' in *Street v. Mountford* gave Mrs Mountford exclusive possession of her room. The case can therefore technically be limited to agreements which confer exclusive posses-sion. Nevertheless, the House of Lords also cast doubt on the effectiveness of 'non-exclusive licences' by disapproving of *Somma v. Hazelhurst* and similar decisions of the lower courts. The Lords considered that in these cases exclusive possession existed in reality, and that the agreements were nothing more than shams. (According to one law lord, the couple in Somma, for example, were intended

in reality 'to live together in undisturbed quasi-connubial bliss'.)
This is not to say that all 'non-exclusive licences' are leases. If a
'non-excusive licence' reflects the reality of the situation – that is,
that the occupier is to share a room, flat or house with unknown
persons or with the landlord – then a licence will have been created.
But if, as is more usual, the reality of the situation is that the
occupier is to rent the accommodation alone or with a friend (or
friends), then the so-called 'non-exclusive licence' will probably be
held by the court to be a tenancy.

future tactics
It would be a foolhardy landlord who tried to evade the Rent Act by
creating a new letting under a non-exclusive agreement. There are
other avoidance devices expressly provided by the legislature which
the landlord can employ (notably the resident landlord let, the
holiday let, the owner-occupier exemption, the retirement exemption and the shorthold tenancy – all described later in the book).

As for existing agreements, an occupier who now believes he has
become a Rent Act tenant as a result of *Street v. Mountford*, has a
choice of tactics. He can either apply for a declaration in the county
court under section 141 of the Rent Act 1977 or he can set out his
claim to a tenancy in a letter to his landlord and if the landlord tries
to take possession proceedings, use that letter as a defence. Alternatively, if the rent is high, he may apply to the rent officer to register
a fair rent. The rent officer can deal only with tenancies within the
Rent Act. Even if the landlord challenges the rent officer's jurisdiction, the rent officer is obliged to enquire into the facts and will
register a rent if he is satisfied that a protected tenancy exists. (The
subject of registering a fair rent is dealt with in detail later in this
book.)

lodgers and 'shams'
If the landlord provides attendance and services (such as laundered
bed-linen and room cleaning) which require the landlord to have

unrestricted access to the premises, the residential occupier is a lodger; he does not have exclusive possession and so cannot be a tenant (this, too, was decided in *Street v. Mountford*). Guests in hotels, bed and breakfast establishments and inmates of nursing homes are clearly all within the 'lodger' category and so is an occupier of a rented room in an old people's home getting meals and the services of a resident housekeeper there.

It is as yet uncertain how wide the term 'lodger' may turn out to be. In a very recent case, *Crancour Ltd v. Silvaesa, 1986*, a couple moved into a bed-sittingroom under a 'licence agreement' which required them to vacate the room with their possessions daily between 10.30 a.m. and noon. The landlord had an absolute right of entry to provide attendance, namely a housekeeper, cleaning of the room, to provide laundered bed-linen, and remove rubbish. The county court judge was satisfied that this was a 'lodging' arrangement. However, the Court of Appeal felt that the landlord had not proved that he was entitled to possession (that is, that the agreement was a licence) and referred the case back to the county court for a full trial on points not brought for appeal. All the three judges involved in the case thought parts of the agreement were 'astonishingly extreme' and pointed towards a sham, in particular the clause limiting rights of occupation to twenty-two and a half hours per day. But they did remark, in passing, that had the agreement represented the true state of affairs between the parties, it would have created a licence.

The court also made it clear that where an agreement contains sham or ungenuine terms, the effect is not automatically to render the whole agreement null and void: the bogus terms are struck out and the remainder of the agreement then examined to see whether exclusive possession is granted.

rent

Rent is not vital to the existence of a tenancy. However, if no rent is paid, this usually indicates that the parties lacked any intention to enter into legal relations, so that the arrangement will be a licence.

summary

The present law relating to the lease/licence distinction is summarised in this chart:

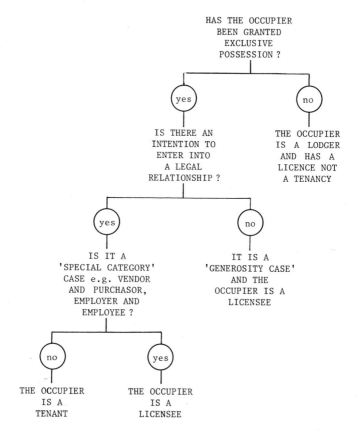

HAS THE OCCUPIER
BEEN GRANTED
EXCLUSIVE
POSSESSION ?

yes — no

yes: IS THERE AN INTENTION TO ENTER INTO A LEGAL RELATIONSHIP ?

no: THE OCCUPIER IS A LODGER AND HAS A LICENCE NOT A TENANCY

yes — no

yes: IS IT A 'SPECIAL CATEGORY' CASE e.g. VENDOR AND PURCHASOR, EMPLOYER AND EMPLOYEE ?

no: IT IS A 'GENEROSITY CASE' AND THE OCCUPIER IS A LICENSEE

no — yes

no: THE OCCUPIER IS A TENANT

yes: THE OCCUPIER IS A LICENSEE

creating a lease

A lease for a term of three years or less may be created orally (by word of mouth) or in writing. This includes a periodic tenancy, even though it may in fact continue for much longer than three years by being automatically renewed. For a lease for over three years to be effective at law, it must be created by deed. A deed is a formal written document which must be 'signed, sealed and delivered'. It only becomes operative when these three requirements have been satisfied.

A lease for more than three years that has not been created in the proper manner (lawyers say 'lacks formality') may nonetheless be enforceable against the landlord as 'an agreement for lease'.

This phrase includes a lease which simply lacks formality (that is, a written lease that is not legal because the document is not a deed) and also a contract that the landlord will grant a lease to the tenant which has not been completed by the execution of a formal lease by deed. Provided it is just in all the circumstances to do so, the court will order the landlord to grant the tenant a proper legal lease on the terms already agreed. Until this is done, the tenant is treated as having a legal lease so that all the agreed terms are binding on both parties. An agreement for lease is sometimes called an 'equitable lease'. This is because originally an agreement for lease was only enforceable in the Court of Equity, a special court which administered a body of rules ('equity') separate from the ordinary law. Nowadays law and equity are administered by the same courts.

Even if there is only an oral grant or agreement, the court will treat it as a grant of a legal lease if the tenant has partly performed the agreement (as long as it is just in all the circumstances to order the landlord to perform his promise). The tenant will have done so if he has entered into possession of the premises and started paying rent. But, of course, this will only work if there is sufficient proof of an oral agreement to grant a lease in the first place.

registration of equitable lease
The courts are willing to enforce an equitable lease but it needs to be protected in the meantime, otherwise a person who later buys the landlord's interest (the reversion) will 'take free' from the equitable lease – that is, he will not be bound by that lease. This protection is achieved by registration by the tenant.

An equitable lease of unregistered land must be registered as an 'estate contract' which is a type of land charge; if of registered land, a notice or caution has to be entered against the landlord's title. The Land Charges Department at Plymouth (telephone Plymouth 779831) will tell you how to register a land charge; the Central Land Registry in London (telephone 01-405 3488) how to lodge a notice or caution.

In the case of registered land, registering an equitable lease is less vital, because an 'equitable' tenant who is in occupation of premises at the time of a later sale will have what is known as an 'overriding interest' and a purchaser who has not enquired of him whether he has any rights in those premises will be bound by that overriding interest and will take the premises subject to the equitable lease – that is, he cannot get rid of the equitable tenant.

getting only a periodic tenancy

Even where there is neither a properly created legal nor an equitable lease, the tenant still gets something. The law presumes that a tenant who goes into possession of property and pays rent periodically has a periodic tenancy, measured by when he pays the rent. Thus, if he pays rent monthly he has a monthly tenancy; weekly, a weekly tenancy; yearly, a yearly tenancy. And because it is for under three years, it can be legal even though created orally. Such a tenancy will most probably be protected by the Rent Act, so that even though the tenant has not got quite what he bargained for, he does have the very real advantages of security of tenure and controlled rent. If the tenancy falls outside the Rent Act, however, the tenant is in a vulnerable position. Although his periodic tenancy, being legal, will bind subsequent purchasers of the reversion, it can be terminated by the landlord, or his successor, giving one month's notice if rent is paid weekly or monthly; by six months' notice if rent is paid yearly.

It is better for a lease for even under three years to be in writing, rather than created orally, because this may avoid argument on a number of points, in particular those to be dealt with in the next section of this book.

creating a licence
There are no formal requirements for the creation of a licence. It helps to have writing, so that the terms of the licence are clear, but a licence does not have to be in writing. And being in writing does not make it a lease: it may still be only a licence.

repair and maintenance

The following comments relate in the main to leases only. A licensor-landlord has to repair and maintain the premises himself. The agreement may exempt him from responsibility for repairs, where, for example, the property is due to be redeveloped and the licence is granted on the basis that the licensee is being allowed in for a short time, in the present state of the premises, in effect because the premises are in such a poor condition. But for an ordinary property, not scheduled for redevelopment, if the occupier is obliged to repair, the likelihood is that the arrangement is in reality a lease, not a licence.

covenants to repair

A lease may contain express provision (that is, a covenant) about the repairing obligations of either party or both parties. It is quite common for the repairing obligations to be shared, so that the landlord is responsible for external repairs and the tenant for internal repairs.

A tenant who covenants 'to repair' does not have to remedy defects which are already in the premises when the lease is granted. One who covenants 'to keep in repair' or 'to put and keep in repair' has to do any repairs that are necessary at the beginning of the lease.

A tenant's covenant may except 'fair wear and tear'. The effect of this exception, which is often found in short leases, is to relieve the tenant from liability for disrepair arising both from natural causes, such as age and weathering, and normal and reasonable use by the tenant for the purposes for which the premises are let. But the tenant has to do such repairs as are necessary to prevent the consequences of the wear and tear producing other consequences which would not normally result from wear and tear. Lord Denning explained in

Regis Property Co Ltd v. Dudley, 1959: "I have never understood that in an ordinary house, a fair wear and tear exception reduced the burden of repairs to practically nothing at all. It exempts a tenant from liability for repairs that are decorative and for remedying parts that wear or come adrift in the course of reasonable use, but it does not exempt him from anything else. If further damage is likely to flow from the wear and tear, he must do such repairs as are necessary to stop that further damage. If a slate falls off the roof through wear and tear and in consequence the roof is likely to let through the water, the tenant is not responsible for the slate coming off but he ought to put in another one to prevent further damage."

If the premises are damaged by fire, the established rule is that if the tenant is responsible for repairs, he must go on paying the rent and re-build the premises (unless the lease states otherwise).

If the tenant covenants to repair, the landlord usually reserves the right to enter the premises and view the state of repair.

If the landlord covenants to repair, he has an implied right to enter the premises to view the state of repair and to effect repairs. But unless he actually knows about the defect, he is liable to repair only if the tenant gives him notice of the disrepair.

Difficult questions can arise as to the meaning of 'repair' in either a landlord's or tenant's covenant. The general rule is that 'repair' may involve the replacement or renewal of parts but not renewal or improvement of the whole or substantially the whole of the premises.

In the last resort, the court will decide whether or not work that needs doing falls within a tenant's covenant, and any dispute will have to be settled by the court, by reference to the particular covenant.

no covenants to repair

If there is no express provision in the lease, the law implies a duty on the part of the tenant to repair, but the extent of this depends on the length of his lease. A weekly or monthly tenant has no duty to repair as such, but must not deliberately change the character of the premises (so he cannot make any alterations) and must use them in a 'tenant-like' manner. He must, as Lord Denning said in *Warren v. Keen, 1954* "take proper care of the place. He must, if he is going away for the winter, turn off the water and empty the boiler. He must clean the chimneys, when necessary, and also the windows. He must mend the electric light when it fuses. He must unstop the sink when it is blocked by his waste. . . . But apart from such things, if the house falls into disrepair through fair wear and tear or lapse of time, or for any reason not caused by him then the tenant is not liable to repair it." A yearly tenant must probably also keep the premises wind- and water-tight, fair wear and tear excepted.

A tenant for a fixed term of years is under a higher duty in that he must do such repairs as are necessary for him to be able to give up the premises at the end of the term in the same condition as he acquired them.

At common law, there is no implied obligation on the landlord either to put the premises into a state of repair at the beginning of the term of the lease, or to do repairs during the term. There are, however, exceptions to this general rule. First, a landlord who lets a furnished house impliedly warrants that the house is fit for human habitation when let. If this is not the case because, for example, the house is bug-infested or the lavatories are not working properly, the tenant can repudiate (end) the tenancy and claim damages for any loss he has suffered. But if the house is fit for habitation when let, the landlord need do no more: he does not have to keep the house fit for habitation.

Second, the landlord who owns and lets flats in a high-rise block may be under a duty to maintain essential communal facilities, such as lifts.

Thirdly (under section 8 of the Landlord and Tenant Act 1985), where a house or part of a house is let at a low rent, there is an implied condition by the landlord that the house is fit for human habitation at the beginning of the tenancy and an implied undertaking by the landlord that he will keep it in this condition throughout the term. This is, however, rarely of use to residential tenants because the rent limits are extremely low – less than £80 in London and £52 elsewhere. And fourthly, section 11 of the Landlord and Tenant Act 1985 imposes important repairing obligations on landlords who grant short leases of dwelling houses, including flats.

repairing obligations in short leases
Landlords, especially local authorities, rarely covenant to repair in residential leases; statute has therefore intervened – but only with regard to short-term tenancies. Section 11 of the Landlord and

Tenant Act 1985 (formerly section 32 of the Housing Act 1961) applies to any tenancy created on or after 24 October 1961 which, when granted, was for a term of less than seven years, including periodic tenancies. It imposes on the landlord the duty to repair the structure and exterior of the building. This covers anything (including drains, gutters, external pipes) that can be regarded as an essential integral part of the structure or exterior of the flat. Thus, repair of the roof would come within the landlord's liability towards the tenant of a top floor flat.

It is important to realise that the structure or exterior must be in disrepair, not just of faulty design. In a case which was decided in 1985 (*Quick v. Taff – Ely Borough Council*), the tenant and his family lived in a council house which had bad condensation, caused partly by lack of insulation in the windows and sweating from the single glazed metal window frames. The sitting room was unusable and the condensation had damaged the decorations, furniture and clothes. The Court of Appeal found that the council were not liable to replace the metal window frames under their obligations under the Landlord and Tenant Act. The window frames were badly designed but neither they nor any other part of the structure or exterior of the house was in disrepair: it was the interior that was in disrepair.

Section 11 of the Landlord and Tenant Act further places on the landlord an obligation to keep in repair and proper working order the installations in the dwelling house for the supply of water, gas and electricity and for sanitation (including basins, sinks, baths and w.c.'s, but not other fixtures, fittings and appliances for making use of the supply of water, gas or electricity) and for space-heating and heating water.

The installation may have to be replaced by the landlord if it is not in proper working order because of some design fault. In *Liverpool City Council v. Irwin, 1976*, the lavatory cisterns in a block of flats flooded because of faulty design. The House of Lords ordered the council to replace them: "Bathroom equipment which floods when it should flush is clearly not in 'working order', leave alone 'proper' working order. . . . To say that such whimsical behaviour is attributable to faulty design is to advance an explanation which affords no excuse for the clear failure 'to . . . keep in proper working order'. The council could be liable to replace it if it could not be modified to function satisfactorily."

In the above cases, the landlords happened to be the council, but the same principles apply equally to private landlords.

Section 11 does not make the landlord liable for repairs as a result of the tenant's failure to use the premises in a tenant-like manner, nor does it make the landlord liable to repair after damage or destruction by fire or other unavoidable accident.

If the landlord is responsible for repairs under the section, he or an agent authorised by him in writing may, at reasonable times of the day and provided he gives the tenant 24 hours notice in writing, enter the property to inspect the state of repair.

The parties cannot contract out of section 11 without the permission of the county court – in other words, the section applies whatever the lease says.

other laws affecting landlord's duty

There are other statutory provisions which affect a landlord's liability to repair. The Occupier's Liability Act 1957 provides that where the landlord retains part of a building under his control (common entrances, for instance), he owes a duty of care to the tenant and his visitors. The Occupier's Liability Act 1984 imposes a similar duty on a landlord towards trespassers and those entering the premises under a contract, for example service engineers and workmen. The Defective Premises Act 1972 states that if the landlord has an obligation or right to repair, he owes a duty to anyone who might reasonably be affected by the lack of repair.

tenant not meeting his repairing obligations

If the tenant breaks his covenant (express or implied) to repair, the landlord has two choices: he may sue for damages to compensate him for the deterioration in the state of the premises, or he may forfeit the lease. But the landlord may not re-enter the premises and carry out the repairs himself, nor may he ask the court for an injunction or for an order of specific performance to force the tenant to carry out the repairs.

forfeiture

Forfeiture is a redress the landlord has if the tenant is in breach of a covenant (here, covenant to repair, but it applies equally to breach of other covenants) which involves bringing the lease to an end. The lease must, however, expressly give the landlord the right to forfeit: the right is not implied. A typical forfeiture clause will state that if the rent is in arrear for 21 days or if the tenant is in breach of any of his covenants, the landlord can re-enter, that is, retake possession of, the property and end the lease.

There is a special procedure which the landlord must follow if he wants to forfeit the lease on breach by the tenant of any of his covenants (including repair) other than for payment of rent.

First, he must serve on the tenant a notice called a 'section 146 notice' (because it deals with matters contained in that section of the Law of Property Act 1925) which

(i) specifies the breach (in the case of a repairing covenant, this is usually done by preparing a schedule of dilapidations);
(ii) requires it to be remedied;
(iii) asks for compensation, if this is desired.

The tenant must be allowed a reasonable time to comply with the notice. If he does not comply, the landlord can proceed with the forfeiture, by bringing a possession action in the High Court or, more usually, serving a county court notice of intention to seek possession.

It is unlawful (under section 2 of the Protection from Eviction Act 1977) to enforce a right of re-entry and forfeiture otherwise than by proceedings in court, while anyone is lawfully residing on the premises. The county court has jurisdiction to hear an action for possession where the rateable value of the premises at the time of the proceedings is £1,500 or less in London and £750 or less elsewhere (most residential lettings will fall within the county courts' jurisdiction).

The Consumer Publication *Taking your own case to court or tribunal* includes a section on possession cases both from the landlord's point of view and that of a tenant defending a claim for possession.

The tenant has the right to apply to the court for relief, that is not to have his lease forfeited. But he must make his application before the landlord regains possession of the premises. This relief will be granted if it is just and fair in all the circumstances and subject to such conditions as the court thinks fit. In the case of a repairing covenant, the tenant may, for example, be told to do the repairs within a certain period.

A sub-tenant is also affected: if the tenant's lease is ended, his lease goes too. A landlord must inform any sub-tenant when he commences proceedings for forfeiture against his tenant. A sub-tenant has the same right to apply to the court for relief as the tenant. He must do so before the landlord re-takes possession from the tenant, that is during the proceedings against the tenant. If the tenant does not ask for, or is not granted relief from forfeiting his lease, but a sub-tenant is, the sub-tenant will then be entitled to remain in possession. He will be given a new lease direct from the landlord for the rest of the term and on the same conditions as his sub-lease. (It may be that he has first to fulfill the tenant's repairing obligations.)

restrictions on the landlord's remedies for breach of repairing covenant
Where the tenant breaks his repairing covenant, the landlord's remedies of forfeiture and damages are not unrestricted. Various statutes intervene.

internal decorative repair
Section 147 of the Law of Property Act 1925 gives the court power to relieve the tenant from internal decorative repairs if, having regard to all the circumstances of the case (in which the length of the lease is an important factor), it is of the opinion that the landlord is acting unreasonably in requiring the repairs to be done. Section 147 does not apply to a breach of covenant to put the premises in repair at the beginning of the tenancy, but can be used in proceedings for forfeiture or an action for damages.

the court's permission needed
Section 1 of the Leasehold Property (Repairs) Act 1938 (as amended by the Landlord and Tenant Act 1954) applies where the lease is for at least 7 years, of which at least 3 years are still to run.

Its net effect is to prevent the landlord seeking forfeiture or suing for damages for breach of a repairing covenant without the express permission of the court. The procedure is that the landlord must first serve on the tenant a 'section 146 notice' which, as well as containing the usual information, must tell the tenant that he has a right under the Leasehold Property (Repairs) Act 1938 to serve a counter-notice (that is, send a letter saying he claims the benefit of the 1938 Act) within 28 days. If the tenant does so, the landlord needs the permission of the court to proceed and this may only be given on one of five specified grounds, for example, if immediate repair is necessary to comply with a local authority bye-law or if immediate repair would be cheap compared to the expense if repair were postponed.

amount of damages
The landlord is precluded, by section 18 of the Landlord and Tenant Act 1927, from recovering an amount of damages greater than the sum by which the value of the reversion (the landlord's interest at the end of the lease) has decreased as a result of the breach of the repairing covenant.

tenant trying to enforce landlord's covenant to repair

If the landlord (private individual or a local authority) breaks his covenant to repair, the tenant may take any one or more of the following steps.

(i) *claim damages*
Recent court decisions show that the tenant may be able to claim by way of damages
  ○ the cost of the repairs (where the landlord refuses to repair altogether)
  ○ the reasonable cost of having to take alternative accommodation while the repairs are being carried out
  ○ a sum for the inconvenience and discomfort of occupying dilapidated accommodation

○ any loss of rent which the tenant may have suffered by not being able to sub-let (provided the landlord knew of this intention to sub-let)

○ any loss of capital value where the tenant is forced to sell because of the landlord's default

○ the cost of redecoration once the repairs have been done.

(Recovering damages presupposes a successful court action. The problems with taking a landlord to court include the uncertainty, delay and expense involved.)

(ii) *ask the court to order the landlord to repair*

(In legal language, this is to ask for an order of specific performance. But this remedy is 'discretionary': the court does not have to order the repair; whether they do is likely to depend on how seriously the lack of repairs affects the tenant's health, for example, and whether in their view financial damages would provide adequate compensation.)

(iii) *do the repairs himself and deduct the cost from future payments of rent*

(However, the tenant should proceed with caution, otherwise he might find the landlord bringing an action for rent arrears and perhaps even for possession. First, the tenant must be sure that there has been a breach of the covenant to repair and, secondly, warn the landlord that he intends to withhold the rent and use it to carry out the repairs. To be on the safe side, he should seek advice from a citizens advice bureau, housing aid or law centre. It is advisable to obtain two or three estimates for the repairs and send copies to the landlord.)

(iv) *ask the court to appoint a receiver (a court official) to collect the rent and carry out repairs*

So far, this has only been done in connection with large blocks of flats, where the disrepair was serious.

(v) *ask the local authority to require the landlord to carry out the repairs.*

This remedy has the advantage of saving the tenant the cost and time of bringing court proceedings, and distancing him from the landlord.

The Secure Tenancies (Right to Repair Scheme) Regulations 1986 allow some public sector tenants the right to recover the cost of undertaking certain repairs.

invoking Public Health and Housing Acts legislation to get repairs done

Local authorities have extensive powers available to them to deal with statutory nuisances in their areas. The main provisions are found in the Public Health Act 1936 ('the 1936 Act'), the Public Health (Recurring Nuisances) Act 1969 and the emergency provisions under the Building Act 1984. Although these powers are designed to be used by local authorities, a tenant may also take private action against a landlord or a local authority under the 1936 Act.

There is a general duty, under the 1936 Act, for local authorities to inspect their districts 'from time to time' in order to ascertain whether statutory nuisances exist. The local authority must take action if a statutory nuisance has been revealed as a result of a general survey or after an inspection has been carried out in response to a complaint.

The tenant can go direct to the local authority's environmental health officer. If he is not there, make an appointment for him to come in person to the house to have a look. It is part of his job. If he finds accommodation in a state which is 'prejudicial to health' or a statutory nuisance, with defects that need to be remedied urgently, the local authority must make the landlord fix it. The local authority can serve the landlord with an 'abatement notice', under the 1936 Act, requiring him to carry out certain works to abate the nuisance, within a specified period. An abatement notice is served on the person by whose 'act, default or sufferance' the statutory nuisance exists (which may be the owner or occupier; in the case of a structural defect, the notice is served on the owner).

If the work is not done on time, the authority must take out a summons against the landlord in the magistrates' court. If the justices are satisfied that the accommodation is a statutory nuisance they will make a 'nuisance order'. This again requires the landlord to do the work, and gives a time limit. The landlord can be fined for failure to comply with a nuisance order, plus a further fine for each subsequent day on which the statutory nuisance continues.

This procedure, based on the Public Health Acts, is quite lengthy. Some complaints which could be dealt with using this procedure may also be acted upon by the local authority using Housing Act legislation: there is a potential for overlap between the Public Health and the Housing Acts.

urgent or emergency cases

Delays resulting from the use of the summary procedure render it inappropriate in cases of statutory nuisance requiring urgent remedy. These cases may involve, for example, a complaint of penetrating dampness caused by a leaking roof and the subsequent collapse of damp ceiling plaster in a room. In such a case, unreasonable delay would be caused if the summary procedure were invoked.

If the local authority thinks that the abatement notice procedure will not work, it may (under section 76 of the Building Act 1984) serve the landlord with a nine-day notice. The landlord would have nine days to carry out the required works specified in the notice. If the landlord does not start the repair work, or at least make clear his intention of starting the work within 9 days, the local authority may carry out the work themselves and subsequently recover their costs from him. Should the landlord wish to prevent this happening, he must serve a 'counter notice' stating that he intends to do the required work. If the landlord says he intends to carry out the work but takes his time over it and does not start within a reasonable time, the local authority may also carry out the work themselves.

This procedure is particularly useful because tenants may be able to suggest that urgent action should be taken to make the landlord carry out repairs quickly under threat of an emergency nine-day notice being served.

recurring statutory nuisance

The Public Health (Recurring Nuisances) Act 1969 can be used by local authorities where a statutory nuisance has existed in the past and is likely to recur. In such cases, the local authority may serve a 'prohibition notice'. This may specify the remedial works required to prevent a recurrence of the statutory nuisance. The same provisions which apply to the abatement procedure apply here. This procedure is useful in cases where the statutory nuisance occurs intermittently, for example with certain drainage problems or penetrating dampness which occur during periods of prolonged and frequent rainfall, commonly during the winter months when low temperatures exacerbate a problem which is not apparent in the summer.

unfit for human habitation

Part VI of the Housing Act 1985 contains several provisions regarding 'fitness for human habitation'. If the local authority considers that a 'house' (which includes all residential accommodation) is unfit for human habitation because of its bad state of repair (instability, dampness, faulty water supply, drainage and sanitary installations, lack of facilities for preparing food and disposing of waste water, etc) and work to bring it up to standard can be carried out at a reasonable cost, the local authority must serve a notice on the landlord. This notice states what work is necessary to make the house fit and gives a reasonable time, not less than 21 days, in which the work should be finished.

If the local authority appears to be refusing to consider whether a house is unfit for habitation, the tenant can request a Justice of the Peace to visit the house. If the JP feels that the house is unfit for human habitation, he can then make a complaint to the local authority; the local authority must then immediately inspect the house.

Where the justices find that the statutory nuisance renders the premises unfit for human habitation, they may make a nuisance order prohibiting the use of the premises for habitation until such time as they are made fit.

Under Part VI of the Housing Act 1985, where a house is not quite unfit for human habitation but in substantial disrepair, having regard to its 'age, character and locality', the local authority may serve a notice on the landlord specifying the substantial repairs required to bring the house up to standard. A reasonable period of time must be stipulated within which the person having control of the premises must carry out the works. If the notice is not complied with, the local authority may carry out the work itself and charge the landlord.

multiple-occupation house

If a local authority feel that a landlord is not managing a house (flats are included) in multiple occupation properly they can, under the Housing Act 1985, require the landlord to carry out repairs and generally improve the management of the house. Where they consider it so bad that the only way of improving the conditions for the tenants is for the local authority to take over the management of the house in multiple occupation, they can make a management order. Broadly, the regulations require a manager of a house in multiple occupation to ensure repair, maintenance, cleaning and good order of water supplies and drainage, kitchens, bathrooms and water closets in shared use, sinks and wash-hand basins in shared use, common parts and outbuildings, yards and gardens in shared use. Also, satisfactory arrangements for refuse and litter disposal should be made.

If the living conditions in the house in multiple occupation are such that the tenants' safety, welfare or health need to be protected, a control order may be made by the local authority. This carries special powers which enable the local authority to have the right of possession of the premises and to take over the management. Such orders are infrequently made, and are normally followed by a compulsory purchase order.

In addition to these measures, local authorities also have powers to control overcrowding and may request the landlord to provide proper means of escape in case of fire, and to ensure that the premises are suitable for the number of people accommodated, to ensure that there ar sufficient facilities and amenities for the tenants. A local authority normally has a code of practice for houses in multiple occupation which sets out the expected standards.

getting advice

The legislation exists but, in practice, enforcement may not be easy. SHAC (The London Housing Aid Centre, 189a Old Brompton Road, London SW5 0AR) suggests as sources of advice:

○ **A housing aid centre:** Your council may have one or you can get a list from SHAC.
○ **A local law centre:** The Law Centres Federation – telephone 01-387 8570, can tell you where your nearest one is.
○ **A neighbourhood advice centre** or other local community advice centre.
○ **A citizens advice bureau:** Look in the telephone directory to find the address of one in your area. Even if they cannot help they should be able to refer you to an agency which can.

protection from harassment and the threat of eviction

Section 1 of the Protection from Eviction Act 1977 gives important protection to the 'residential occupier', that is a person occupying premises as a residence. Occupation may be under a contract or by virtue of any enactment or rule of law which gives him the right to remain in occupation or restricts the right of anyone else to recover possession of the premises. So, provided his residential occupation is lawful, a tenant or licensee is protected – but an unwelcome guest, a licensee whose contract has ended, a trespasser or squatter is not.

Two offences are established by section 1. First, it is an offence for anyone, including a landlord or his agent, unlawfully to deprive a residential occupier of his premises or any part of the premises.

It is a defence for the landlord to show that he genuinely believed, and had reasonable cause to believe, that the occupier had ceased to live on the premises. It is therefore important for a tenant or licensee who is threatened with eviction to state clearly that he intends to continue living at the premises and he should make sure that he does not stay away from the flat for long periods without leaving his everyday possessions there.

Second, it is an offence, known as harassment, for the landlord to do anything calculated to interfere with the peace or comfort of the residential occupier or members of his household, or persistently to withhold services (for example, water, gas or electricity) that are reasonably required for the occupation of the premises, with intent to cause him to give up the premises or to stop him from exercising any of his rights in respect of the premises.

Proving harassment is not easy; threats and abuse are obvious examples and so is cutting off of services (persistently, not just once) turning off the water or electricity, for example. Other examples of harassment would be changing the locks, letting gas or electricity meters jam up, throwing out belongings, allowing a pop group to rehearse in the next-door flat, writing threatening letters and issuing a 'notice to quit' without justification, not cleaning common parts, or offering payment to the tenant to give up possession.

One of these acts can be sufficient to constitute harassment; there do not need to be several if the tenant's peace and comfort is interfered with. Moreover, the act may be committed by someone acting on behalf of the landlord, not necessarily directly by the landlord. However, it must be proved that it was the intent of the harasser to force the occupier out or stop him from doing something he was entitled to do.

For example in one recent case heard by the courts, the tenant refused an offer of alternative hotel accommodation while the landlord carried out repairs to her room. Then the ceiling of her room fell down due to the repairs that were being carried out, so she had to move out anyway. She brought an action against the landlord for harassment but was unsuccessful because she could not prove that the landlord had caused the ceiling to fall down deliberately to force her out.

invoking the courts
Unlawful eviction and harassment are criminal offences: a tenant should report offences of this nature to the local authority's harassment officer.

At present, the maximum penalty for contravening section 1 of the Protection from Eviction Act is a fine of £1,000 and/or 6 months in prison (or if there has been a trial by jury, an unlimited fine and/or 2 years in prison). In addition, the court can order that compensation (of up to £2,000) be paid to the occupier if he suffered personal damage from the offence for which the landlord is convicted.

It is also possible for the occupier to take civil action by suing the landlord. The conduct complained of will probably be a breach of the covenants or agreement between the parties, for example the term implied in all tenancies (and expressly stated in some) that the tenant is allowed quiet enjoyment of the tenancy. Or the landlord's conduct may give rise to an action in trespass (for example if the landlord enters the premises without permission). In appropriate landlord enters the premises without permission). In appropriate cases, the tenant may be granted an injunction against eviction or future harassment or an order for reinstatement. The landlord may be ordered to pay the tenant 'aggravated' or 'exemplary' damages, as a sign of how seriously the court views the landlord's conduct. In one case, the tenant was locked out of his house by his landlord after he (the tenant) had applied to the rent officer to get the rent lowered. By the time he had got a reinstatement order from the court (that is an order forcing the landlord to let him back into possession of the house), the house was in a terrible mess. The landlord was ordered to pay him £1,000 'exemplary' damages.

The SHAC booklet *Private tenants: protection from eviction* summarises what protection from eviction means and suggests that a tenant who is unsure of the degree of protection he has should contact a local law centre, or housing aid centre, neighbourhood advice centre or a solicitor for further advice.

regulated tenancies

The majority of residential lettings by private landlords are regulated tenancies under the Rent Act 1977 as amended by the Housing Act 1980. A regulated tenancy is mainly distinguished from others by where the landlord lives and who he is. If he lives in another dwelling, or is a property company, the tenancy is almost always regulated. In addition, for a tenancy to be regulated, the tenant must pay enough rent, but not for food and services, and the rateable value of the property must be below a set figure.

A regulated tenancy gives to a tenant the protection of controlled rent and security of tenure. Here is a summary of the more important consequences of a regulated tenancy.

○ The landlord cannot regain possession of the accommodation without a court order, and the court may only grant an order in prescribed circumstances.

○ When the tenant dies, the tenancy will usually pass to a member of his family who has been living in the accommodation.

○ The court may order the transfer of a regulated tenancy from one spouse to another when a decree of judicial separation or divorce is granted, or at any time afterwards.

○ The landlord and the tenant, together or separately, can apply to the rent officer for a fair rent to be registered.

○ If no rent is registered, the parties are free to agree a rent, provided certain formalities are observed. There is no limit on the rent the parties can agree.

○ If a fair rent is registered, that is the maximum rent the landlord can charge until it is properly changed.

○ The tenant has rights in respect of any variable service charge he pays.

Regulated tenants also are able to enforce the rights theoretically available to all tenants, for example rights to repair, or to quiet enjoyment of their home, without risking eviction as a result of their actions.

definition

The definition of a regulated tenancy has three component parts. There must be:

(i) a dwelling-house
(ii) which is let
(iii) as a separate dwelling.

(i) a dwelling-house
'Dwelling-house' has been interpreted very widely by the courts. It includes a house or part of a house, a cottage, bungalow, maisonette or flat, a single room (for example a bedroom or bed-sit), even a beach-hut – in short, any building which is capable of being lived in. Two flats let together as one dwelling may constitute a dwelling-house, and so may a house and an adjacent cottage which are let together. The premises may be furnished or unfurnished.

(ii) which is let
There must be a tenancy: the relationship of landlord and tenant must exist. A licence to occupy cannot be a regulated tenancy. Thus lodgers, caretakers and employees who have to occupy accommodation because of their job are excluded. It does not matter how the tenancy was created, whether by deed, written agreement or by word of mouth, nor whether it is a periodic tenancy or a tenancy for a fixed term.

(iii) as a separate dwelling
It must be intended at the time of the letting that the tenant should live in the accommodation. If the letting is for some other purpose, a shop for instance, then it is not a regulated tenancy. One tenant

who used to sleep in his antique shop, failed in his claim to be a regulated tenant. The letting was for the purpose of his antiques business.

The accommodation must be let as a single unit. This normally means that the tenant must be able to sleep, cook and eat there. It seems that washing is a secondary aspect of living – the fact that a tenant has to share bathroom facilities with others does not prevent a regulated tenancy from arising. One dwelling-house may comprise several single units, let separately; but if all the accommodation in the dwelling-house is shared, there is no letting of a separate dwelling. Furthermore, two self-contained units (for example two flats) may constitute one separate dwelling if let as such.

exceptions

The letting will not be a regulated tenancy if one (or more) of the following twelve exceptions applies:

(i) If the rateable value of the property is above the rateable value limits laid down by the Rent Act 1977. The way in which the limits are defined by section 4 of the Act is complicated, but broadly speaking a property will be within the rateable value limits if its present rateable value is £1,500 or less in Greater London, or £750 or less elsewhere. If the present rateable value of a property is higher than this, it may still come within the rateable value limits if its rateable value on the valuation list which expired on 31st March 1973 was £600 or less in Greater London, or £300 or less elsewhere. The local authority's valuation officer will help with enquiries relating to rateable values.

(ii) If no rent is payable, or the rent is a low rent. The rent payable under the tenancy must be not less than $\frac{2}{3}$ of the rateable value on 'the appropriate day'. 'The appropriate day' is either 23 March 1965 if the property was rated at that time or, if not, the date on which it became rated. In this context, rent means the whole rent payable to the landlord, including rates and quantified service charges. Long leaseholders (that is, whose lease is for 21 years or more) are usually excluded from being regulated tenants because they pay little or no rent; their payments for rates, services, maintenance or insurance are not counted for this purpose.

A tenant can gain or lose the protection of the Rent Act if there is a change in the terms of his tenancy. One rather obvious, but effective, move of a landlord who wishes to free himself of a regulated tenant is to offer that tenant a new lease at a very low rent, namely less than two-thirds of the 'appropriate day' rateable value. A tenant should therefore think very carefully before accepting such a seemingly attractive offer.

(iii) If part of the tenant's dwelling-house is licensed for the sale of intoxicating liquor for consumption on the premises. A publican letting a flat above his pub, however, can do so on a regulated tenancy.

(iv) If the rent includes payment for board or attendance. As far as attendance is concerned, the exclusion only operates if the payment for it forms a substantial part of the rent.

Board means 'prepared food served on the premises'. An early morning cup of tea would not count; continental breakfast probably would (but providing breakfast in another building will not). Landlords sometimes go to great pains to bring themselves within this exception – perhaps spending the early hours of the morning leaving plates of steaming eggs and bacon on the doorsteps of numerous tenants. The court has not yet had the opportunity to give a ruling on whether the provision by the landlord of weekly groceries constitutes 'board'.

Attendance means 'services personal to the tenant' and would include cleaning rooms, doing laundry and changing bed-linen, but not the cleaning of communal parts, such as entrance hall and stairways.

(v) If the letting is by a university, college or polytechnic to one of its students, or by some other body specified by regulation. The bodies are all educational institutions and foundations specifically established to provide accommodation. This is relevant to students and the people who rent from these bodies while the accommodation is not required for students; with 'out of student-term' lettings, the tenant has to move out of the accommodation at the end of the term.

(vi) If the purpose of the letting is to confer on the tenant the right to occupy the dwelling-house for a holiday. Holiday means 'a period of cessation of work, or period of recreation'. It has not yet been finally decided by the courts whether premises let for the purposes of a working holiday can come within the exception. The letting must be a genuine holiday let, not a sham. So, for example, a landlord cannot genuinely intend to let for the purposes of a holiday when he knows the occupiers are student nurses. If the agreement contains a statement that it is a holiday letting, it would be up to the tenant to prove to the court that the expressed purpose is a false label.

(vii) If the property is let for business or mixed residential and business purposes.

(viii) If the landlord is a local authority, a housing association or housing co-operative.

(ix) If the landlord is a government department. Lettings by the Crown, however, are capable of being regulated tenancies, provided the property is managed by the Crown Estates Commissioners (which most Crown property is) and the letting does not fall within one of the other exceptions.

(x) If the letting is an assured tenancy.

(xi) If the tenancy was granted after 14 August 1974 by a resident landlord. A 'resident landlord' is one who lives in the same house or flat as the tenant and has done so from the time the tenant moved in. Living in the same block of flats (as against in the same flat) would not make him a resident landlord. But a landlord living in another flat in a converted house would be a resident landlord. A company landlord (that is a company which owns and lets out premises) cannot 'reside'. Although a resident landlord must be resident in the property at the time of the letting, he may have more than one home and need not occupy any of them continuously. But he must always intend to return and use the property as a home and show visible signs of that intention, such as leaving clothes there.

Before 1974, the distinction was between furnished and unfurnished tenancies, rather than resident and non-resident landlords. Furnished tenancies were excepted from protection. It may be necessary to decide whether a tenancy created before August 1974 was furnished or unfurnished, because if it was unfurnished, it will still be a regulated tenancy even though there is a resident landlord.

(xii) If the landlord is not resident but shares living accommodation with the tenant (a kitchen or sitting-room; sharing a w.c. or bathroom does not count).

company tenants

'Company lets' (where the tenant is a company) are a semi-exception to regulated tenancies. A limited company tenant can claim Rent Act protection as far as rent is concerned but it cannot claim security of tenure either for itself or for a resident occupier. The letting must genuinely be to a company. A tenant may challenge a 'company let' on the ground that its expressed purpose is a sham, if he can show that in reality the accommodation was meant for him alone, not for employees (or a certain type of employees, such as company directors) generally.

disputes

If there is any doubt whether or not a regulated tenancy has been created, either the landlord or the tenant may apply to the county court for a declaration as to the status of the letting. A tenant would be wise to seek legal advice before embarking on this. If the court finds against him, not only will he be putting his home at risk, but will incur court costs. It may be better for him to await possession action by the landlord and then attempt to establish a regulated tenancy as part of the defence.

protected and statutory tenancies

A regulated tenancy may be either protected or statutory. It is protected while the original agreement, written or oral, is in existence. When the protected tenancy comes to an end, provided the tenant goes on living in the accommodation, what is known as a statutory tenancy will arise on the same terms and conditions as originally agreed (in so far as they are consistent with a statutory tenancy).

This statutory tenancy confers no interest in land on the tenant; it is merely a personal right to remain in occupation and will last only as long as the tenant remains in residence. As a consequence, the tenant cannot normally assign (that is, sell) or sub-let the whole of the premises. (Also, if a statutory tenant goes bankrupt, the trustee in bankruptcy gets nothing because the tenancy is not assignable, and the tenant is entitled to remain in his home. But if a protected tenant goes bankrupt, the original agreement is still in existence and the tenancy passes to the trustee in bankruptcy and the tenant may have to move out.)

This does not mean that a statutory tenant can never leave his home, and it is recognised that a person can have more than one home. As Lord Justice Asquith said in *Brown v. Brown, 1948*: "To retain possession . . . for the purpose of retaining protection, the tenant cannot be compelled to spend 24 hours in all weathers under his own roof 365 days in the year. Clearly, for instance, the tenant of a London house who spends his weekends in the country, or his long vacation in Scotland does not necessarily cease to be in occupation. Nevertheless absence may be sufficiently prolonged or intermittent to compel the inference . . . of a cesser of possession or occupation."

Generally speaking, the tenant must at times use the accommodation as his home and, if away, always intend to return and leave visible signs of that intention, such as clothes, furniture or a member of his family with whom he normally resides. Thus a tenant, with a house in the country, who stayed in his flat twice a week, but rarely ate a meal there, succeeded in his claim to a statutory tenancy. Similarly, a tenant who left his flat in order to care for his seriously ill parents, but always retained a wish to return to the flat permanently, retained his statutory tenancy. In another case, however, a statutory tenant of a flat went to live with his girlfriend although he left clothes and furniture in the flat and used the flat during the day to work (he was a writer); he lost his statutory tenancy.

Where either a husband or wife is entitled to occupy accommodation by virtue of a statutory tenancy, as long as the other spouse is there that counts as occupation by the tenant, for the purposes of keeping the statutory tenancy alive. The landlord cannot refuse to accept rent from whichever spouse is in occupation. (This prevents the landlord bringing proceedings to end the tenancy on the ground of non-payment of rent.)

successors

On the death of the original tenant, whether still protected or statutory, the tenancy is automatically transferred as a statutory tenancy to a 'first successor' and on the death of the first successor to a 'second successor'. When the second successor dies, the statutory tenancy comes to an end.

who is the 'first successor'?

Provided the tenant's husband or wife was living in the property immediately before the tenant died, he or she will be the first successor. If this does not apply, the first successor can be any member of the tenant's family who was living with the tenant during the six months preceding his or her death. If more than one relative qualifies, and succession cannot be decided between the relatives by agreement, the county court can be asked to decide.

A 'second successor' succeeds in exactly the same way, namely the first successor's surviving spouse, then a resident relative.

who is a member of the tenant's family?

'Any member of the tenant's family' is not defined by the Rent Act, but it is clear that the word 'family' is not confined to its traditional meaning (mother, father, in-laws, children, grandchildren, brothers, sisters, uncles and aunts, and so on). Case law has rendered it flexible enough to embrace, for example, adopted children, illegitimate children and a so-called 'common-law' wife or husband. There must however have been a familial link between the tenant and the claimant, for these purposes, and platonic relationships between adults do not count, nor non-familial relationships between persons of the same sex.

an anomaly

A protected tenant owns an interest in land which on his death will pass in the normal way to the person entitled under his will or intestacy. But that person's entitlement to the protected tenancy may be suspended, possibly for the lifetime of two successors, if a transmitted statutory tenancy is claimed by a resident spouse or relative.

Example: In 1975, Paul Turner, a widower, got a flat with a twenty year lease that will come to an end in 1995. He lives there with his sister Sarah. In 1987 he dies without having made a will. Under the intestacy rules his property, which includes the lease of the flat, goes to his daughter Diana. But Sarah can, and does, stay on – as the first successor under a transmitted statutory tenancy. Her niece Nora moves in with her, and on Sarah's death Nora becomes the second successor, again under a transmitted statutory tenancy. Only on Nora's death would Diana's entitlement become effective but not if the period of the original lease has come to an end (i.e. after 1995).

divorced and separated spouses

Under the Matrimonial Homes Act 1983, the court has power on granting a decree of divorce, nullity, or judicial separation, or at any later time, to make an order transferring a protected or statutory tenancy from one spouse to the other. The landlord has no right of veto, merely a right to be heard by the judge at the time of the divorce, and the needs of the non-tenant spouse (and children) must be balanced against the position of the landlord; his objections will be overridden if necessary. The court's jurisdiction under the 1983 Act does not extend to unmarried couples.

getting vacant possession

A landlord cannot get vacant possession from a regulated tenant unless, if the tenancy is still protected, he ends it in the proper manner and obtains a possession order from the court. For this, he must establish one of the grounds for possession set out in the Rent Act.

ending a protected tenancy

If the tenancy can be ended by notice to quit, either because there is an express term to this effect or because the tenancy is a periodic one, at least four weeks' notice in writing must be given to the tenant. The period of notice will have to be longer if the lease so requires, or if the tenancy period is for more than four weeks. A notice to quit a periodic tenancy must expire at the end of a complete period of the tenancy (for example at the end of the week, if weekly) unless the tenancy agreement states otherwise.

notice to quit

A notice to quit must contain the following prescribed information (in the following recommended form of words):

'1. *If the tenant does not leave the dwelling, the landlord must get an order for possession from the court before the tenant can lawfully be evicted. The landlord cannot apply for such an order before the notice to quit has run out.*

'2. *A tenant who does not know if he has any right to remain in possession after a notice to quit runs out or is otherwise unsure of his rights, can obtain advice from a solicitor. Help with all or part of the cost of legal advice and assistance may be available under the Legal Aid Scheme. He should also be able to obtain information from a Citizens Advice Bureau, a Housing Aid Centre, a Rent Officer or a Rent Tribunal Office.'*

Standard *Notice to Quit a Dwelling* forms are available from law stationers.

When a protected tenant receives a notice to quit, he does not have to get out there and then. He does not need to leave unless and until the landlord has obtained a possession order from the court.

no notice to quit

It is rare for a lease for a fixed term to have a clause allowing the landlord to terminate it by notice to quit; the lease comes to an end automatically on the specified date and cannot be ended sooner. But most fixed term leases contain a provision allowing the landlord to forfeit the lease if the tenant fails to pay the rent or breaks any of his other covenants. (Some periodic leases also contain a forfeiture clause, although this is unusual. Since notice is so easy to give to bring a periodic agreement to an end, such a clause would rarely, if ever, be used.) A landlord must first serve the tenant with a 'section 146' notice before proceeding to forfeit the lease for breach of covenant other than non-payment of rent. And whatever the breach (non-payment of rent or otherwise), the landlord must get a court order for forfeiture.

The landlord cannot bring proceedings for possession under the Rent Act until the fixed term lease ends, or he forfeits. Technically he must first bring forfeiture proceedings, then separate proceedings for possession. Forfeiture proceedings are a separate matter from other court proceedings for possession under the Rent Act. But because the same grounds will generally be used for both, it is more convenient that they be heard together; they will normally be brought at the same time, so that the court can consider whether or not the tenant should be allowed to remain in possession in the light of the various Rent Act grounds for possession and the tenant's right to relief.

When a protected tenancy has been ended in the proper manner (by notice to quit in the case of a periodic tenancy; expiry or forfeiture in the case of a fixed term tenancy), a statutory tenancy arises and the landlord can apply to the court for a possession order.

No notice to quit is necessary in the case of a statutory tenancy. But the landlord would need a court order for possession before the tenant needs to move out.

obtaining a court order for possession

The circumstances under which a court (usually the county court) may or must grant an order for possession are laid down by law, in section 98 and schedule 15 of the Rent Act 1977 (as amended by the Housing Act 1980 and the Rent (Amendment) Act 1985). Most of the statutory grounds for possession are called 'cases'. Cases 1 to 10 under Part I of schedule 15 are discretionary (case 7 has been abolished by the Housing Act 1980); cases 11 to 20 under Part II are mandatory.

If the landlord can show that one of cases 11 to 20 under Part II applies, then the court must order possession. The court does not have to consider whether it is reasonable to make the order.

In all other situations, the landlord must satisfy the court both that it is reasonable to make the order and that either

○ suitable alternative accommodation is available; or
○ the circumstances are as specified in any of cases 1 to 10 under Part I.

reasonableness
The Rent Act gives no definition of the word 'reasonable' but case law has established that in considering reasonableness the court should take into account:

○ the purpose of the Rent Act, which is to confer security of tenure
○ the personal circumstances of both parties, landlord and tenant, including their financial and housing positions, their ages and health
○ the tenant's conduct under the tenancy, for example whether rent payments are regular or irregular
○ the severity of any breach of covenant
○ public interest.

suitable alternative accommodation
The court may make an order for possession if it is satisfied that it is reasonable to do so and that suitable alternative accommodation is available to the tenant, or will be available to him when the order for possession takes effect. (Some of the cases suggest that it is less difficult to show 'reasonableness' where alternative accommodation is offered.)

There are two ways in which a landlord can show the existence of suitable alternative accommodation. Firstly, he can produce a certificate from a local housing authority certifying that they are providing the alternative accommodation. Local authorities rarely give such certificates. Secondly, he can find and offer alternative accommodation himself. This accommodation will be suitable if:

   (i) it gives the tenant equal or equivalent security of tenure;
     and
  (ii) it is reasonably convenient as regard the tenant's and his or her family's place of work;
     and
 (iii) the rent and size of the accommodation are that which a local authority or court would consider suitable for the needs of the tenant and his or her family;
     and
 (iv) where appropriate, similar or suitable furniture is provided;
     and
  (v) the character of the property is suitable to the tenant's and his or her family's needs.

This last requirement was recently considered by the Court of Appeal in *Hill v. Rochard, 1983*. A retired couple were statutory tenants of The Grange, a period country house with a large number of rooms, servants' quarters, outbuildings, stables, a large garden and about one and a half acres of land. The landlords bought, for £52,000, a four-bedroomed modern detached house with a garden and garage near to The Grange, and offered it as alternative accommodation to the couple. The offer was refused. The court granted an order for possession. In assessing the suitability of alternative accommodation, the court has to look at the tenant's needs, not his particular wishes and desires. The house clearly satisfied the couple's housing needs, if not their wishes.

However, a differently constituted Court of Appeal took a different view in *Battlespring Ltd v. Gates, 1983*, in which an elderly widow was offered as alternative accommodation a similar flat to her present accommodation. But she had lived in her present flat for 35 years and had an emotional attachment to it and the Court of Appeal, agreeing with the county court judge, held that it would not be reasonable to make the order.

discretionary grounds for possession

The cases in which the court may make an order for possession if it also thinks it reasonable to do so but where no alternative accommodation is offered, are as follows:

CASE I

The tenant has not paid the rent or is in breach of one of his other obligations in the tenancy agreement – for example, to repair. The court can suspend the operation of a possession order on conditions, for example that the tenant pays off all arrears of rent, or does the necessary repairs.

(The order to pay off the arrears should only be made if it would not cause exceptional hardship to the tenant; tenants on supplementary benefit can argue that exceptional hardship would be caused.)

CASE II

The tenant has caused a nuisance or annoyance to neighbours (not necessarily adjoining but in the near vicinity) *or has been convicted of using the premises for illegal or immoral purposes.*

In general, the nuisance must be proved to be serious. Persistently playing loud music would constitute 'nuisance or annoyance', as would receiving late callers at frequent intervals. A conviction for receiving stolen goods or of being in possession of cannabis resin on the premises would be relevant under the second part of 'case II'.

CASE III

The tenant has damaged the property or allowed it to deteriorate (except for fair wear and tear).

In *Holloway v. Povey, 1984*, an order for possession was granted to a landlord against a tenant who adamantly refused to mow the lawn and who let the grass grow uncontrolled. The order was suspended on condition that the tenant would tidy up the garden and keep it tidy for one year.

CASE IV

The tenant has damaged furniture that was provided by the landlord (except for fair wear and tear).

CASE V

The tenant gave notice to quit (but subsequently changed his mind) and in consequence of the notice the landlord has contracted to sell or let the property. The landlord would need to show that the tenant not leaving would cause him financial loss.

CASE VI

The tenant has assigned or sub-let the whole of the property without the landlord's consent. This is only appropriate to a protected tenancy; a statutory tenant who assigns or sub-lets the whole of the property puts the tenant outside the protection of the Rent Act.

CASE VIII

The tenant was an employee of the landlord and the landlord now reasonably requires the accommodation for a new employee.

CASE IX

The landlord reasonably requires the property as a home for himself or member of his immediate family. To grant an order for possession under this case, the court must be satisfied that greater hardship would be caused by refusing the order than by granting it.

The landlord has to show that he reasonably requires the property as a home for himself or a member of his family and that it is reasonable to make the order for possession, but it is up to the tenant to show greater hardship. All the relevant circumstances are taken into consideration in deciding whose would be the greater hardship, including: availability of other accommodation, financial status, health, others who would be affected (for example dependants), length of time the tenant has lived in the area, job and school connections in the area, and so on.

The court may make an order for future possession, as it did where a 62-year-old landlord wanted possession of a tenanted cottage so that she would have somewhere to live on her mother's imminent death.

Case nine is not available at all to a landlord who bought the premises with the regulated tenant already in occupation, but is available if he became the landlord in some other way, for example because he inherited the property, with a sitting tenant in it.

CASE X
The tenant has charged a sub-tenant a higher rent than is permitted. This applies only where there is a rent registered for the premises, or part of them, with the rent officer or by a rent tribunal.

mandatory grounds for possession

These are listed in Part II of Schedule 15 to the Rent Act. There are also ten. If the landlord establishes any of the grounds detailed in cases XI to XX, the court is obliged to grant him a possession order, irrespective of whether it thinks it reasonable to do so.

To be operative, each case requires the landlord to have given 'notice in writing to the tenant that possession might be recovered under this case', no later than the start of the tenancy (before the grant of the tenancy, in the case of a shorthold). But this requirement may be waived and a possession order granted by the court in cases XI, XII, XIX and XX provided it thinks it just and equitable to do so. It is not yet authoritatively decided whether it is sufficient for the landlord to give such a notice by word of mouth.

There is a special procedure enabling landlords to get possession quickly under cases XI to XX. The county court office can advise on how to do this (and will help applicants to complete forms and explain exactly the steps to be followed). A tenant faced with such proceedings has to act fast if he wishes to oppose the landlord's application: the period between his receiving the court papers and the hearing will be at most 14 clear days, instead of the usual 21 days – it may, in some cases, be as little as 7 days.

Once a mandatory order for possession is made, it cannot be postponed for more than 14 days except on the grounds of exceptional hardship. If there is exceptional hardship, the court can postpone the order for up to six weeks. Exceptional hardship is a question of fact in each case – for example, if the tenant or a member of his family has some sort of special need, like no stairs because of severe arthritis, it may take a little longer than two weeks to find somewhere to live.

Here are the ten mandatory cases:

CASE XI *returning owner-occupiers*
(This case has been amended by the Rent (Amendment) Act 1985, which applies to case XI lettings whenever they were granted.) It is designed to enable a person to let his home temporarily.

Provided the landlord lived in the accommodation at some time before letting it and, from the start of that tenancy and previous ones, gave written notice to the tenant that possession might be recovered under case XI, the court will order the tenant to move out if it is satisfied regarding one of the following:

(1) the owner-occupier or any member of his family who was living with him when he last occupied the accommodation, wishes to live in it; or

(2) the owner-occupier has died and a member of his family who was living with him when he last occupied the accommodation (or another house) wishes to live in it; or

(3) the owner-occupier has died and the person who has inherited the reversion either wants to live in it or sell it with vacant possession; or

(4) the property is subject to a mortgage and the lender wishes to exercise his power of sale (for example because repayments have not been made); or

(5) the owner-occupier wants to sell the property with vacant possession in order to buy a home nearer his work.

It is not necessary for the landlord to have lived in the accommodation immediately before the letting. Therefore, a landlord who occupied the house as his residence some years before the present tenancy, or who granted a succession of case XI tenancies culminating in the present one without going back into residence before each, will be entitled to possession, provided the other conditions are satisfied.

And if it considers it just and equitable to do so, the court can still grant an order for possession, even though the owner did not serve the proper notice.

In practice, it can be safer even where case XI would apply, for the landlord to retain out of the lease a bedroom in the house or flat and a right of access to it, so that if he returns from his absence abroad, say, he can still at least have access to a room in the house while the court proceedings are going ahead.

An 'owner-occupier' does not have to be the freeholder: a tenant who is entitled to sub-let the whole of his home under his agreement can also use case XI in order to get possession from his sub-tenant.

The Department of the Environment Housing booklet No 5 *Letting your Home or Retirement Home* is a guide for home owners and servicemen who want to let their homes temporarily.

CASE XII *retirement homes*

This case can be used by people who let a home to which they plan to retire. The owner must intend to live in the accommodation when he retires from regular employment and must have given the tenant notice in writing on or before the start of the tenancy that possession might be required under case XII. If the owner has previously let the property, it must also have been under case XII. The court must order the tenant to give up possession if it is satisfied that:

(1) the owner has retired from regular employment and wants to use the property as a retirement home; or
(2) the owner has died and a member of his family who was living with him at the time of his death, wants to live in the property; or
(3) the owner has died and a person who has inherited the property either wants to live in it or sell it with vacant possession; or
(4) the property is mortgaged and the lender wishes to exercise his power of sale.

The court may waive the requirement that proper notice must be served or that any previous letting must have been under case XII.

CASE XIII *out of 'holiday season' lettings*

This case deals with the problem of what to do with holiday homes out of season. If the home was let for a fixed term of 8 months or less, having been let for a holiday during the previous twelve months, the landlord must be granted a possession order.

Suppose A has a seaside bungalow near Great Yarmouth which he lets out to holidaymakers during the season. From May to October he let the bungalow to Mr. and Mrs. X on a genuine holiday let. No one seems to want to spend money on a seaside holiday there during the winter, and instead of leaving the bungalow empty for the winter months, A decides to let Fred, the local postman, rent it. As long as he first serves Fred with written notice that possession might be recovered under case xiii, and he does not grant Fred a lease for longer than 8 months, he will be able to get a (mandatory) possession order from the court to get Fred out again, because the bungalow was genuinely let for a holiday during the 12 months prior to the lease to Fred.

CASE XIV *out of 'student term' lettings*
This is similar to case xiii. It allows the accommodation owned by educational institutions to be let while it is not required for student use. The accommodation must have been let to the present short-term tenant, the one against whom the educational institution now wants to get possession, for a fixed term of 12 months or less, having been let to students during the previous twelve months.

CASE XV *clergy lettings*
The court must order possession if the accommodation was intended for a clergyman but was temporarily let to an ordinary tenant.

CASE XVI *farmworker lettings*
Similarly, possession will be granted to a farmer who lets property that is usually occupied by a farm worker to an ordinary tenant on a temporary basis.

CASE XVII *farmhouse lettings*
This applies where a landlord requires a farmhouse not previously occupied by a farm manager following amalgamation proposals.

CASE XVIII *farm manager lettings*
This case covers the situation where the accommodation was previously occupied by a farm manager or his widow and has been let temporarily to an ordinary tenant.

CASE XIX *shorthold tenancies*
(Shorthold tenancies are dealt with separately later in this book.)

CASE XX *lettings by servicemen*
This case is similar to cases xi and xii: where a person was a member of the armed forces when he bought and let the property, and the tenant and any previous tenant was given notice on or before the

start of the tenancy that possession might be recovered under case xx, the court must grant an order for possession if it is satisfied that:

(1) the serviceman wants to live in the property; *or*
(2) a member of his family who was living with him at the time of his death, now wants to live in the property; *or*
(3) a person who has inherited the property either wishes to live in it or sell it with vacant possession; *or*
(4) the serviceman needs to sell the property with vacant possession to buy a home nearer his work; *or*
(5) the property is mortgaged and the lender wishes to exercise his power of sale.

The court may waive the 'proper notice' requirement if it thinks it just and equitable to do so.

statutory overcrowding
The court will also grant an order for possession if the property falls within the definition of being overcrowded under Part X of the Housing Act 1985.

tenant ending a regulated tenancy

How a tenant can do this depends on whether the regulated tenancy is protected or statutory.

If the tenancy is still protected and is a

(a) *periodic tenancy* – the tenant must give the landlord at least four weeks' notice to quit, expiring at the end of a complete period of the tenancy (for example the end of a week if the tenancy is weekly). The notice must be in writing but no special form is required. If the tenancy agreement provides for a longer period of notice to be given, the tenant will have to comply with this.
(b) *fixed term tenancy* – the tenant may only end a fixed term tenancy prematurely if either the agreement or the landlord allows him to do so.

If the tenancy has become statutory, the tenant must give the landlord at least four weeks' notice to quit, in writing, but more if the terms of the original agreement require longer notice to be given. Where the original tenancy was for a fixed term, the tenant must give at least three months' notice in writing irrespective of the length of the original fixed term. There is no special form for a tenant's notice to quit a statutory tenancy. Again, the landlord may agree to the tenant leaving without giving notice.

private (non-statutory) agreement

The landlord and the tenant may come to an agreement that the tenant should vacate the premises in return for some financial compensation. Such an agreement is perfectly legitimate, but where a tenant refuses to go through with the deal, the landlord can enforce it only by obtaining a possession order from the court. For this reason, the only way that a completely watertight agreement for the surrender of a statutory tenancy can be made is by getting a consent order for possession from the court. The idea is that the tenant consents formally to the landlord regaining possession, and the court approves the arrangement and embodies it in an order.

However, the court has no jurisdiction to make a consent order for possession except in accordance with section 98 and schedule 15 of the Rent Act – under one of the 'cases'. So for a consent to be effective, the tenant must admit, in the order, either that he does not have the protection of the Rent Act (for example, because he has lost his statutory tenancy through non-residence) or that he is within one of the grounds on which the court can order possession.

In practice the parties generally resort to a more informal method: cash handed to the tenant just as the tenant is leaving. The tenant will obviously not leave unless he is certain to get the money, whereas the landlord will not part with the money unless he is sure of getting vacant possession.

Although this method enjoys a high success rate, there is nothing to prevent the tenant seeking a reinstatement order from the court on the ground, for example, that the landlord forced him into accepting the money payment and leaving.

Whichever method, consent order or cash-in-hand, the amount of compensation payable to the tenant is up to the parties to decide. In some cases, substantial payments are made because the property is far more valuable to the landlord vacant than occupied.

rent control

Security of tenure is not the only advantage of a regulated tenancy. The amount of rent the tenant has to pay may be limited to what is known as a 'fair rent'.

A fair rent is one assessed by a rent officer or, on appeal, a rent assessment committee, in accordance with the rules laid down in the Rent Act 1977. Once assessed, the rent is entered in the rent register which is kept by the rent officer and is open to public inspection, free of charge if you go in person (but if you want to obtain a copy of an entry on the rent register the fee is £1). By looking at rents registered for similar dwellings in the area, a landlord and a tenant can get an idea of the fair rent attributable to their accommodation.

getting a fair rent registered

Either the landlord or the tenant of any regulated tenancy, or both of them together, or the local authority, may apply to the local rent officer for a fair rent to be registered. The address of the rent officer is in the telephone directory.

Application is made on form RR1, available on request from the rent officer, law centres, citizens advice bureaux, housing aid centres. The form is easily completed and asks, amongst other things, for details of the landlord and tenant, a description of the premises and the terms of the tenancy (a copy of any written agreement should be included), whether or not services and furniture are provided and whether a fair rent has been previously registered for the premises.

The rent (including an amount for services and/or furniture provided by the landlord, but exclusive of rates) which the applicant seeks to have registered must be entered on the form. If no rent is specified, the rent officer cannot deal with the application. If the applicant is the landlord, a copy of the application is sent to the tenant, and vice versa.

The parties are usually asked if they wish to meet the rent officer for a consultation. If so, a meeting will be arranged for a few weeks hence. Shortly before the meeting, the rent officer may inspect the premises, accompanied by the parties if they so desire.

The rent officer then decides on a fair rent. Section 70 of the Rent Act requires that in doing so he should have regard to the character, state of repair and locality of the dwelling and if the tenancy is furnished the quality and condition of the furniture. He should disregard any value arising from a shortage of rented accommodation in the area. The value of any improvements made or paid for by the tenant should also be disregarded. The personal and financial circumstances of the landlord and tenant must also be ignored.

Section 70 says nothing about the method a rent officer should use to determine a fair rent. Two methods have been used in the past. The first is the 'comparables' method – that is, using as a starting point fair rents already registered for similar accommodation in the area. The second is the 'contractor's theory' which involves calculating a percentage return on capital values. It is generally thought that the 'comparables' method favours tenants, the 'contractor's theory' landlords. Many tenants and many landlords would deny that either is particularly beneficial. Nowadays, most rent officers use the 'comparables' method.

The resulting fair rent will be registered about six to eight weeks after the initial application was received. Both parties will be sent a copy of the registration sheet, together with copies of the rent officer's papers on the case and notes outlining the effect of the registration.

The Organisation for Private Tenants (Unit 201, 444 Brixton Road, London SW9 8EJ) is bringing out a booklet *A pocket guide to rent registration* which sets out the procedure step by step.

the service element

A registered rent reflects the cost of any services provided by the landlord, for instance, porterage and cleaning. Details of the cost of any services have to be entered on the application form by whoever is making the application, and can be challenged and must be substantiated if the tenant or rent officer so requires. If a 'fixed' fair rent is registered, such part of it as is attributable to services is noted separately (unless it is less than 5% of the total rent) and so is any increase in the cost of services since the previous rent. The amount of any increase called the 'service element' of the registered rent is not subject to the rules about phasing the increase.

Often a tenancy agreement provides that the landlord may vary any service charge payable. If the rent officer approves this provision, he will register a rent which reflects, but does not detail, the current cost of services, and state that the fair rent is 'variable'. This means that a landlord can recover the actual amount expended on services for any particular period of time. How this amount is split among different flat owners in a block depends on the agreement between the landlord and the flat owners. Sometimes the charge is split pro rata according to the size of each flat, sometimes it is just split equally.

Sections 18 to 25 of the Landlord and Tenant Act 1985 give protection to a tenant who has to pay a variable service charge. The landlord can only recover service charges to the extent that they are reasonably incurred and, if they are incurred on the provision of services or the carrying out of works, only if the services or works are of a reasonable standard. The county court has the power to make a declaration as to these matters. The landlord cannot recover service charges in excess of what is reasonable. So if the tenant pays what he thinks is reasonable, the landlord will have to get a court declaration if he wants more. If the tenant is wrong, he will not only have to pay up, but also pay the legal costs of the case.

The tenant has the right to obtain a summary of the costs on which any service charge was calculated and to inspect the receipts on which the summary is based.

Further, if the tenant is liable to contribute towards the cost of repairs, he has the right to be consulted before the landlord carries out any repair work. In certain cases of more major repairs, the landlord must obtain at least two estimates for consideration by the tenant, one of which must be from a person, firm or company wholly independent of the landlord.

The landlord who fails to comply with these obligations commits an offence punishable by a fine.

The Department of the Environment's booklet *Service Charges in Flats* gives an outline of the provisions in the Landlord and Tenant Act 1985 regarding variable service charges. It also describes the provisions (in section 59 of the Housing Act 1980) which apply if you pay for services as part of a fixed rent registered by the rent officer.

no rates element

A registered rent does not include rates. If the landlord pays the rates, he cannot recover them from the tenant unless the tenancy is statutory or the tenancy agreement so provides. In any other case, the landlord will have to wait until the protected tenancy has ended before he can begin to charge for rates. A periodic protected tenancy can be ended by notice to quit. However, instead of the landlord having to serve both this and a demand for rates, the law allows him to serve a *Notice of increase of rates* which fulfils both purposes. The length of the notice (that is the date of the increase) must be for the same length as a notice to quit and cannot be backdated. When the notice has expired, the periodic protected tenancy ends and a statutory tenancy comes into being. From then on, the landlord can charge for rates.

certificate of fair rent

Prospective landlords can discover what a fair rent for their premises would be by applying for a certificate of fair rent. New developers and landlords intending to carry out improvements to tenanted or untenanted premises often avail themselves of this procedure.

Form CFR1 has to be used, available from the rent officer. It requires similar details as form RR1 and asks for the ground of application – whether new dwellings will be created by building or conversion, whether improvements will be made, and whether premises will be let on a regulated tenancy. The rent the landlord wishes to have registered must be specified. The landlord and any tenant can consult with the rent officer and the premises are normally inspected.

An objection can be made to the fair rent which the rent officer proposes to insert in a certificate. If no objection is received (the tenant, if any, is given 14 days to object) the certificate is issued. When the premises are let, or the improvements have been carried out as proposed, the landlord may apply to the rent officer to have the fair rent in the certificate registered. The application must be made within two years of the date the certificate is issued.

objection

If the landlord or the tenant is dissatisfied with the rent registered, he may (within 28 days of receiving notification of the registration) ask the rent officer by letter or in person to refer the matter to a tribunal called the rent assessment committee. A committee is normally made up of three people: a layman, a valuer and a lawyer who acts as chairman. They take a new look at the facts and assess a rent for the premises which they deem fair at the time of their decision – but they, too, are bound by the Rent Act 1977.

An objection cannot be made if:

○ a joint application was made by the landlord and the tenant and the rent officer determined, without further consultation, that the rent specified in the application was a fair one; or
○ the landlord had obtained a certificate of fair rent and the rent registered was the same as the certificate.

When the committee has received an objection, the party objecting is sent a printed explanation (on form RR102) of how his case will be dealt with. Next, a letter (known as RR7H) is sent to both parties asking them whether they wish to make oral or written representations. The letter may also give the date, time and place of the hearing if it has been decided to call one. There is a time limit for replying to RR7H, usually 7 days. Any of the rent officer's papers on the case which were not sent to the parties previously will accompany the letter. At this stage, the committee may ask either party to supply further information. There is a fine if this is not done within 14 days.

If no hearing has been requested (either by the committee or the parties), both parties are given an opportunity to comment on each other's written representations. The committee nearly always inspects the premises before making a decision.

the hearing

If a hearing has been requested, or is ordered by the committee, the parties will be given about 10 days' notice of its date, time and venue, by standard letter (RR8). Hearings are open to the public. The parties may speak for themselves or get someone else to represent them (not necessarily a solicitor).

The course of the hearing depends on who attends. The committee can go ahead with the hearing even though one of the parties does not turn up, provided they are satisfied that sufficient warning was given. The applicant will be called first. If he is the landlord, he will be asked to state his rent proposals and the tenant is given the opportunity to question him. Then the tenant will be asked to present his case, and the landlord is allowed to question him. The committee may also question the parties and witnesses may be asked to speak.

The object of a hearing (and also written representations) is to acquaint the committee fully with the arguments of both sides.

Although the idea of appealing to a tribunal is daunting to most laymen, they should not be overawed. The chairman of the committee is likely to be helpful. He says when the parties should speak and when they should question and is willing to answer any reasonable questions himself.

Both parties should state what they think the rent should be, and why. Relevant points may include the size, age and locality of the dwelling, its state of repair and any furniture and services provided. The shortage of rented accommodation in the area will not be considered by the committee, and the financial and personal circumstances of the parties are irrelevant – for example, where a tenant cannot take advantage of facilities offered and included in rent (such as upkeep of lift for ground floor tenant or use of tennis court for 86-year-old granny). The idea is to be fair to both parties – to assess what would be an objective fair rent for the premises (therefore the scarcity value, which benefits a landlord, is also disregarded).

The committee will confirm the rent officer's figure if it appears to them to be fair. If not, they will determine a fair rent themselves which may be higher or lower, fixed or variable (if the lease allows for a variation). They sometimes give their decision at the hearing but more usually it is communicated through the post (using form RR9). The committee need not, and do not, give reasons for their decision unless one of the parties asks them to do so before the hearing. Their decision is also sent to the rent officer. He then either marks in the register that the rent is confirmed or registers the new rent.

There is a right to appeal to the High Court against a committee's decision on a point of law under section 141 of the Rent Act 1977; but the High Court cannot determine a fair rent for the premises.

It is important to realise that on an objection by either party, the rent can be increased or decreased and both the landlord and the tenant should give careful consideration whether an objection should be made, since either of them may end up worse off than they would have been if they had not made the objection.

withdrawal of objection
When a matter has been referred to a rent assessment committee, either party may withdraw his objection if the other party and the committee agree. However, the committee can continue with the case if they think it is against the public interest to withdraw.

the effect of registering a fair rent

Once a fair rent is registered, this is the maximum rent that the landlord can ask to be paid as from the effective date of the registration. For a rent assessed by the rent officer, the effective date is normally the date of registration; for one that has been determined by the rent assessment committee, it is the date of their decision. A registration remains in force, notwithstanding a change of tenant, or change of landlord, until a new application for registration is made or until the registration is cancelled.

If the fair rent is lower than the rent previously paid by the tenant, the landlord must reduce the rent from the effective date. If the tenant has been paying a higher rent than that already registered, which sometimes happens when a new tenant is unaware that a fair rent has been registered for the premises, he can recover (through a court action) the overpayments made in the past two years.

phasing the increase

If the fair rent is greater than that currently being charged, the increase must be phased and cannot be made all at once. Half the increase plus any 'service element' (that is the difference between present and previous amounts attributable to providing services) is payable straightaway, the other half becomes due one year later.

A registered rent is exclusive of rates, so the previous rent limit should, for phasing purposes, also be exclusive. Since many unregistered rents are inclusive, a sum for rates may need to be deducted before calculating phasing.

Unless the tenancy is still protected and the agreement allows for increases, the landlord must serve a prescribed *Notice of Increase* (available from law stationers) on the tenant before he can claim either phase of the increased rent, but one notice can cover both phases of the increase.

If the tenancy is protected, and the agreement does not allow for increases, the landlord cannot start charging the fair rent until he has ended the tenancy. (He will most probably not be able to do this if the tenancy is for a fixed term, but must wait until the term expires.) A periodic tenancy is usually ended by a notice to quit; but to save the landlord having to serve both notices, a notice of increase can serve two purposes. Provided it is for the same length as the notice to quit, it ends the protected tenancy and enables the landlord to charge the first half of the increased rent.

The only way in which a registered rent may be varied is by applying for a new rent to be registered or for the present one to be cancelled.

applying for a new rent to be registered

A new application for registration cannot be made until two years have elapsed from the date when the last registration took effect, except where:

○ a landlord submits an application for re-registration three months before that date (but any new registration will not take effect until the two years are up); or
○ a joint application is made by the landlord and tenant; or
○ there has been a material change in the condition of the dwelling or in the terms of the tenancy and the registered rent is no longer a fair rent.

cancellation

The landlord and the tenant can apply jointly to have a registered rent cancelled. The application should be made on form RR103 and two years must have elapsed since the effective date of the last registration. The parties must have agreed a new rent and a copy of their rent agreement (which must comply with the rules) should accompany the application. One term of the agreement must be that the landlord cannot end the tenancy (except for non-payment of rent or breach of any other covenant) within 12 months of the application for cancellation. The rent officer can only cancel if he is satisfied that the rent payable under the proposed agreement is a fair one and that any terms for variation of payments for services, maintenance and repair are reasonable. There is no right of appeal from his decision. If he decides not to cancel, the registered rent continues in force.

Once the rent is cancelled, the parties can make further rent agreements. A cancellation stops neither party from later applying to the rent officer to determine a fair rent.

A tenant may be tempted to participate in an application for cancellation if he suspects that the landlord is offering him a lower than fair rent. But the tenant must be sure that this indeed is a lower rent, bearing in mind that a fair rent set by the rent officer would be phased.

A landlord may apply for a cancellation on his own, if two years have elapsed since the effective date of the last registration and the premises are not currently let to a regulated tenant. The prescribed form is form RR104.

new tenancy

When a new tenancy is granted and there was no fair rent registered in respect of the property during a previous tenancy, the parties can agree on whatever rent they choose. Once they have agreed a figure for rent, that figure can only be increased if the tenancy is still contractual (protected) and the agreement so provides or, where the agreement does not allow for increases, by a formal rent agreement. Such an agreement must be in writing, signed by both parties and state 'in characters not less conspicuous than those used in any other part of the agreement' that the tenant's security of tenure under the Rent Act will not be affected if he refused to enter into the agreement, that in any event he may apply at any time to the rent officer for a rent to be registered and that if the increase had been determined on application for registration, then the increase would have been phased.

Housing booklet No 7 *Regulated Tenancies* (issued by the Department of the Environment and Welsh Office) concentrates on explanations of fair rents and security of tenure.

miscellaneous points about regulated tenancies

premiums and associated payments

It is a criminal offence to require or receive a premium or 'key money' as a condition of a grant or renewal of a regulated tenancy or the transfer of it to a new tenant. On conviction, the landlord may be ordered to repay the money to the tenant and is liable to a fine. The payment does not have to be made to the landlord to constitute an illegal premium; it can be made to his agent or to a tenant who is transferring the tenancy.

A premium includes any payment in addition to rent, for example the excess over a reasonable price for furniture. A landlord may, however, take a deposit from a tenant of furnished or unfurnished premises, provided it is not more than one-sixth of the annual rent and is reasonable in relation to the tenant's potential liability.

It is also an offence to require a tenant to pay rent in advance of the rental period it covers (suppose it is a monthly tenancy, the landlord cannot demand December's rent in November but he can ask for it on 1 December) or to pay rent more than six months in advance. The tenant is entitled to recover any rent so paid.

It is not an offence for the landlord to pay the tenant for the surrender of the lease, although any agreement or contract to this effect will be unenforceable.

rent books

The use of a rent book is widespread but the duty on the landlord to provide one is limited; he need only do so where rent is payable weekly.

A rent book is useful because of the information it must contain. It must state the name and address of the landlord and his agent, the address of the premises, the rent and rates payable by the occupier, and the terms and conditions of the tenancy, explain to the tenant his right to security of tenure and rent control, and mention the existence of housing benefit scheme. Rent books can be bought from law stationers.

Failure to provide a rent book is a criminal offence punishable by a fine, but it does not affect the right of the landlord to recover rent properly due to him.

A rent book is a convenient way of bringing to tenants' attention information about their rights under the Rent Act, and it also provides a record of the terms of the tenancy, so reducing the possibility of disputes. The rationale behind the rule that a rent book needs to be provided only where rent is payable weekly is that weekly tenancies are hardly ever in writing and therefore require the protection of a rent book.

details of the landlord
Any tenant who occupies residential accommodation is entitled, under section 1 of the Landlord and Tenant Act 1985, to be supplied with the name and address of his landlord by making a written request to his immediate landlord, the person who collects the rent or the landlord's agent. This information must be given within 21 days (not to do so is an offence with a fine of up to £500).

Where the landlord is a company, the tenant is entitled to have a list of the directors and the secretary.

A new landlord must give details of his name and address to the tenants within two months of acquiring the property. In practice, this generally happens more quickly, because he will have to produce an authority signed by the old landlord (or his agent) that the tenant should pay the rent to him.

sub-letting
A regulated tenant can sub-let unless the terms of his tenancy forbid it. But a statutory tenant who ceases to live in the premises loses the statutory tenancy, so he can only sub-let part. A sub-letting of the whole would be unlawful and the statutory tenant would lose the protection of the Rent Act.

If a tenant sub-lets on a regulated tenancy, he must give his landlord written notice of the sub-letting within 14 days and include details of the occupancy and rent.

The general rule is that if a head tenancy of premises is brought to an end, any sub-tenancy of the whole or any part of those premises ends too. This is not so where a regulated tenant creates a lawful sub-tenancy of the whole or part of the dwelling-house. Under section 137 of the Rent Act 1977, if the regulated head tenancy is ended by possession proceedings, the lawful sub-tenancy does not automatically come to an end. Instead, the sub-tenant of the whole or of any part is deemed to hold directly from the head landlord on the same terms as if the regulated head tenancy had continued. If the head landlord wants possession against the sub-tenant he must bring a separate action.

But section 137 is not without its uncertainties. It is probable that the sub-tenant must himself have been a regulated tenant to enjoy the full protection of the Rent Act. Apparently, section 137 cannot change his rights: all it does is put him into a direct relationship with the head landlord if the head tenancy is terminated. Suppose, then, that the lawful sub-tenant was not a regulated tenant, because the head tenant was a resident landlord. If the head tenancy is ended, section 137 does not alter his rights. Even though the head landlord (now his immediate landlord) is not resident, he is still not a regulated tenant and has no security of tenure.

joint tenancies

A joint tenancy exists where the lease is granted to two or more people (maximum of 4) as legal joint tenants. As far as the landlord and rest of the world are concerned, the position of joint tenants is the same as that of a sole tenant. Each and every joint tenant is responsible for paying the rent and observing the other covenants in the lease. If one joint tenant alone pays the rent or, say, the cost of repairs, he can recover from the other joint tenants. As between themselves, each joint tenant is entitled to exclusive possession of the whole of the premises and no one joint tenant can exclude the other. Joint tenancies can be regulated tenancies in the same way as sole tenancies, if they are of a 'dwelling-house let as a separate dwelling' and do not fall within one of the exceptions laid down by the Rent Act.

The distinguishing feature of a joint tenancy is that when one of the joint tenants dies, his interest 'survives' to the remaining joint tenants, until there is only one survivor left. Where there are joint statutory tenants, the succession provisions in the Rent Act only come into play on the death of the last surviving joint tenant.

If a notice to quit a protected periodic tenancy is served on only one of the joint tenants, it is effectively served on all. The protected periodic tenancy will be followed by a statutory tenancy which can be sustained as long as one of the joint tenants remains in occupation. Where the landlord seeks a possession order against joint statutory tenants, it is sufficient if one of the joint tenants has broken a covenant in the lease or falls within one of the other grounds for possession.

If a joint tenant wishes to leave the accommodation, a newcomer can be made a joint tenant, but there will have to be a new tenancy agreement. A new tenancy agreement will be inferred from the newcomer's name being inserted in the tenancy agreement or rent book.

Problems can arise with informal sharing arrangements, where not all the occupiers' names appear on the lease or where the agreement is oral. There are several possibilities:

- the sharers may all be licensees of the landlord
- the sharers may all be joint tenants
- one may be the tenant (or there may be joint tenants) and the other sharers may be licensees or sub-tenants of the tenant (or joint tenants).

Where the lease names one tenant (or joint tenants) but not all the particular persons, it will be difficult for the other sharers to establish that they are joint tenants. To do so, they will have to prove that the written agreement is a sham. Good evidence that they are really joint tenants would be having been asked for references by the landlord, or having been served with a rent demand. If they are licensees, they have no security of tenure.

Sub-tenant sharers are probably only marginally better off: if, as is likely in the case of sharing arrangements, they have a resident landlord(s), then they too have no security of tenure. And if the head tenancy is terminated, section 137 of the Rent Act (explained above) cannot improve their situation.

controlled tenancies

This type of tenancy no longer exists. A controlled tenancy was one which was protected, before the coming into force of the Rent Act 1965, either under the Rent Acts 1920 to 1938 or under the Rent Act 1939. Its salient feature was that the rent was generally under £2 and could only be increased to take account of the cost of repairs and improvements, and then only by $12\frac{1}{2}\%$ of that cost. Many controlled tenancies became regulated tenancies by operation of the law prior to 1980, and section 64 of the Housing Act 1980 put paid to them finally. All controlled tenancies are now regulated tenancies within the fair rent system.

Now, in 1987, it is extremely unlikely that a tenant would be paying a controlled rent. Obviously it has been in landlords' best interests to apply for a fair rent to be registered immediately a controlled letting became a regulated one, this being the only way of obtaining a realistic rent from the tenant.

A controlled tenancy would have existed before 1980, where:

1 the tenant was living in the dwelling before 10 July 1957 or is the first successor of that tenant (if a second successor, the tenancy would have automatically become a regulated tenancy before 1980); *and*
2 the dwelling was unfurnished and owned by a private landlord; *and*
3 the rateable value of the dwelling on 31 March 1972 was less than £70 in London or £35 elsewhere (if the rateable value was higher the tenancy became regulated by virtue of the Finance Act 1972); *and*
4 the rent was linked to the 1956 rateable value.

The Department of the Environment's booklet *Controlled Tenancies* explains how they were brought into the fair rent system.

Formerly controlled tenancies converted into regulated tenancies by the Housing Act 1980 or under the law prior to that date are otherwise subject to the normal law relating to regulated tenancies.

shorthold tenancies

The shorthold is a form of regulated tenancy introduced by the Housing Act 1980. It represents a move to encourage private landlords to let their property rather than sell it. They can create short lets of dwellings which will be free from the normal security of tenure provisions when the term expires, but still within the fair rent system. A shorthold can be created for a new tenancy only.

When first introduced, a condition to the grant of a shorthold was the compulsory registration of a fair rent. This is still true for lettings in Greater London but not for lettings elsewhere in England and Wales made on or after 1 December 1981.

Any dwelling that can be let on a normal protected tenancy can be let on shorthold. Basically this means that any non-resident private landlord can let furnished or unfurnished accommodation to a tenant on shorthold – provided that he fulfils certain conditions. The tenancy must be:

1 created after 28 November 1980;
   and
2 for a fixed term of between one and five years which cannot be brought to an end earlier by the landlord (unless the tenant breaks one of the terms of the agreement);
   and
3 to a new tenant: although it is impossible to convert the tenancy of an existing protected or statutory tenant into a shorthold, it is possible to offer that tenant a shorthold in some other accommodation, including another flat in the same building or different rooms in the same house. The tenant would be ill-advised to accept such an offer because his security of tenure will be diminished;

and
4 prior to the grant of the tenancy, the landlord has given the tenant a notice in the form prescribed by statute;
   and
5 for all shortholds granted before 1 December 1981 and all shortholds in Greater London whenever created, either
   (a) a fair rent has already been registered by the rent office, or
   (b) the landlord obtains a certificate of fair rent before the grant of the tenancy, and makes an application for the registration of a fair rent not later than 28 days after the start of the tenancy.

Compulsory rent registration is not a condition for shortholds granted on or after 1 December 1981 outside Greater London. If no fair rent is registered for the property, the landlord and tenant are free to agree any rent they choose. Such an agreement does not prejudice either party's right to apply to the rent officer to register a fair rent in the normal way.

the prescribed form of shorthold notice
Failure to comply with the requirement to serve a prescribed form of notice on the tenant (or, where applicable, to comply with the registration of rent requirements), does not totally doom any action for possession by the landlord based on case XIX. These requirements may be ignored by the court if it thinks it just in all the circumstances to do so.

There are different forms of notice for dwellings in Greater London and for dwellings elsewhere. The forms can be bought from law stationers. Both inform the tenant that he is being offered a shorthold tenancy. If the tenant is an existing protected or statutory tenant, he is warned that if he accepts a shorthold tenancy of other accommodation, including another flat in the same building, he will have less security of tenure.

The notice for Greater London details the registered rent, or records the fact that a certificate of fair rent has been obtained by the landlord and that he will be applying within 28 days of the start of the tenancy for the rent specified in the certificate to be registered. In either case, this is the highest rent a tenant can be charged until a higher rent is registered. Any excess paid by the tenant is recoverable (but only going back two years).

The notice for dwellings in England and Wales, not in Greater

London, states the registered rent (if any) and says that this is the highest rent the tenant can be charged. If no fair rent has been registered for the accommodation, the agreed rent should be inserted. This is followed by a statement that either party may apply at any time to the rent officer for the registration of a fair rent.

the rights of the parties during the shorthold term

During the fixed term, the tenant is Rent Act protected as far as security of tenure is concerned. Unless the tenancy agreement provides for forfeiture for non-payment of rent or breach of any of the other terms of the tenancy, the landlord cannot bring the tenancy to a premature end. Any other term giving the landlord the right to terminate the tenancy before the end of the fixed term is not only not effective but turns the tenancy into a fully protected one.

The tenant, on the other hand, has the right to end the tenancy during the fixed term. If the term is for 2 years or less, he must give the landlord one month's notice in writing; if for over 2 years, three months' notice in writing. This right cannot be contracted out of, in the tenancy agreement, and any term which purports to impose a penalty or disability on the tenant if he gives notice, cannot be enforced.

A shorthold tenant may not assign (that is transfer his interest in) the tenancy to someone else. He may, however, sub-let the whole or part of his accommodation – provided that the agreement permits him to do so. But a sub-letting does not affect the landlord's right to regain possession at the end of the fixed term: if a possession order is obtained against a head shorthold tenant, the sub-tenant has to go too (section 137 of the Rent Act does not apply).

The court has power under the Matrimonial Homes Act 1983 to order the transfer of a shorthold tenancy from one spouse to the other, on granting a decree of divorce, nullity of marriage, or judicial separation, or at any time thereafter.

If the tenant dies during the shorthold term, the normal rules of succession under the Rent Act apply: the first successor takes a statutory tenancy which will end on the death of a second successor. Again, the right of the landlord to regain possession still applies.

the rights of the parties at the end of the fixed term

Case XIX, added to schedule 15 of the Rent Act by the Housing Act 1980, gives the landlord a right to possession at the end of the shorthold term, provided he follows the correct procedure. This involves him in two separate stages. First, during the last three months of the shorthold term he must give the tenant at least three months' written notice of his intention to apply for a possession order under case XIX (known as 'the appropriate notice'). Second, he must take proceedings in the county court to obtain possession within three months of the expiry of the appropriate notice.

Provided that the landlord has fulfilled the conditions for creating a shorthold tenancy, has served a valid appropriate notice and taken proceedings within the proper time, the court must grant an order for possession against the tenant. If it thinks it just and equitable to do so, the court may grant the landlord a possession order even if he has not fulfilled certain of the shorthold conditions, namely serving the tenant with a shorthold notice before the grant of the tenancy, or complying with the compulsory rent registration requirement where applicable.

if time limits not observed

If the landlord fails to serve an appropriate notice of his intention to apply for possession under case XIX before the end of the fixed term, or fails to take proceedings within the three month time limit, he still retains the right to possession, but he must wait until three months before the anniversary of the end of the fixed term before he can serve his appropriate notice. So if, for example, the shorthold term ended on 31 December 1984, he could have served his appropriate notice at any time between 1 October and 31 December 1985, or 1 October and 31 December 1986, or can do so between 1 October and 31 December 1987 and so on. Proceedings must be taken within three months of the expiry of the appropriate notice.

The result, from the tenant's point of view, is that he can remain in possession on a yearly basis. Once the fixed term ends (or a successor becomes entitled to the tenancy) however, the tenant becomes a statutory tenant, and all the grounds for possession in

Schedule 15 of the Rent Act become available to the landlord; he can offer suitable alternative accommodation, for instance. Furthermore, whatever the original shorthold agreement said, a statutory tenant cannot sub-let the whole of the premises. If he does, he loses the statutory tenancy.

If, instead of just allowing a shorthold tenant or his successor to 'hold over' (that is, stay on) at the end of the shorthold term, the landlord grants the tenant a new tenancy, at his own or the tenant's option, this new tenancy cannot be a shorthold tenancy because it is granted to someone who was already a protected or statutory tenant. The new tenancy is an ordinary regulated tenancy, but the landlord still retains his right to recover possession under case XIX.

Suppose, for example, a tenant was granted an initial shorthold term of 1 year and was able to renew on a yearly basis (a periodic tenancy). Recovery of the premises by the landlord would be possible on any anniversary of the grant of the term, but if the tenant obtains a periodic tenancy (so becoming an ordinary protected tenant), then recovery of possession by the landlord is possible only after proper notice to quit, plus either a case XIX notice on the tenant or establishing one of the other grounds for possession in the Rent Act.

The housing booklet No 8 *Shorthold Tenancies*, a guide for private landlords and tenants, published by the Department of the Environment, includes specimen shorthold notices.

assured tenancies

To encourage the building of new housing for letting in the private sector, the Housing Act 1980 created an entirely new form of residential tenure called assured tenancies. Assured tenants fall outside the protection of the Rent Act 1977 and instead have security of tenure similar to that enjoyed by business tenants under the Landlord and Tenant Act 1954 Part II. This security is a statutory right to claim a renewal of the lease when it comes to an end, and compensation if a new lease is refused. The attraction of an assured tenancy from the landlord's point of view is that rents are fixed at an open market level. (Nevertheless, to date, only about 500 homes have been let on assured tenancies.)

Four conditions must be satisfied before an assured tenancy can be created. First, the landlord must be not an individual but a body approved by the Secretary of State. So far, several building societies, pension funds, property companies and building companies have been approved. Second, the premises must be newly built: construction work must have been started after 8 August 1980. At present, assured tenancies do not apply to conversions. The third condition is that before the tenant first occupied the property, no part of the premises had been lived in except on an assured tenancy. The last condition is that the tenancy would be a protected (or a housing association) tenancy were it not an assured tenancy. If these conditions are fulfilled, the tenant will be an assured tenant unless he is formally told to the contrary before the start of the tenancy.

The new Housing and Planning Act 1986 proposes to extend the assured tenancy scheme to empty premises where, in the two year period prior to the first assured letting, 'qualifying works' have been

carried out. They could be works of repair, conversion or improvement. The works must have cost more than the 'prescribed amount'
(expected to be at least £5,000; the Secretary of State has to bring
out an order, under the new Act, to prescribe the amount).

rent

There is no control on the rent that can be charged at the beginning
of an assured tenancy: it is for the parties to agree between
themselves. And if an assured tenancy is renewed under the statutory procedure, the rent will be that payable on the open market.

security of tenure

An assured tenant cannot be evicted without a court order. This
means that unless the tenant fails to pay rent or breaks some other
term of the tenancy, and the landlord forfeits in accordance with a
clause in the tenancy agreement, he is entitled to remain in possession. When the original agreement expires, the assured tenancy
continues automatically until either party starts the statutory procedure to end the tenancy.

A landlord who wants to end an assured tenancy at the end of the
term and does not want to negotiate a new tenancy, must give at
least six months' and not more than twelve months' notice in the
prescribed form. If the tenant wishes to remain in his home, he must
write to the landlord within 2 months, telling him so. He must also
apply to the county court between 2 and 4 months of receiving the
notice from the landlord.

A tenant who wishes to end the tenancy must give at least three
months' notice in writing if his tenancy is for a fixed term; if periodic
he must give an ordinary common law notice to quit of at least 4
weeks.

renewal

When the assured tenancy comes to an end, the parties no longer
need to have regard to the statutory procedure and are free to
negotiate and agree a new tenancy. If there is no agreement, and
provided that the landlord has not served a notice, as above, the
tenant has to serve the landlord with a notice requesting a new
tenancy in the prescribed form (in writing, specifying the termination date of the current tenancy and the beginning of the new one,

and proposing terms of the new tenancy) and then apply to the court for a new tenancy. The notice requesting a new tenancy and the taking of proceedings are governed by strict time limits and procedures and the tenant is advised to seek legal advice.

The landlord can oppose the grant of a new tenancy on one or more of the following grounds:

○ disrepair resulting from the tenant not having observed his repairing obligations under the current tenancy (only if the dwelling is in a very bad state of repair and the tenant does not remedy the situation before the date of the hearing)
○ persistent delay by the tenant in paying his rent
○ other substantial breaches by the tenant of the tenancy agreement
○ the landlord having offered the tenant suitable alternative accommodation (either an assured, protected [but not shorthold] or secure tenancy)
○ possession being required so that the whole of the dwelling can be let or disposed of as a single unit
○ the landlord intending to occupy the premises himself, or to demolish or reconstruct the property.

If the landlord cannot establish any of these grounds, the court may order that a new tenancy for up to fourteen years be granted, and has wide discretion as to the other terms of the tenancy.

compensation

If the landlord gains possession on either of the last two grounds above, or does not offer suitable alternative accommodation, he has to pay compensation to the tenant. The amount of compensation is $2\frac{1}{4}$ times the rateable value of the property. Any agreement purporting to exclude the tenant's right to compensation is invalid.

The Department of the Environment's booklet on *Assured Tenancies* provides a general guide for landlords and tenants about their rights and obligations and describes how landlords can become approved bodies to let homes on assured tenancies. It includes specimen forms.

tenancies for mixed residential and business purposes

Lettings of premises which are used for residential *and* business purposes are excluded from protection under the Rent Act 1977. Instead, they come under Part II of the Landlord and Tenant Act 1954 (which, like the Rent Act, applies only to tenancies, not licences). Although the Act defines 'business' widely to mean any trade, profession or employment, in the context of this book, its provisions in the main affect small shops let with living accommodation above.

Sometimes premises are let for residential purposes and then used by the tenant for his business. Whether such activity constitutes the carrying on of a 'business', for the purposes of the 1954 Act, is a question of degree to be decided in the light of all the circumstances. If the tenant takes in lodgers, for example, the number of rooms, size of the establishment, sums involved and services provided, would all be relevant factors.

The tenant's protection is twofold: security of tenure and compensation for displacement. There is no initial rent control. In other words, the mixed residential and business tenant has much the same protection as the assured tenant.

security of tenure
The tenant cannot be made to give up the premises without a court order.

The tenancy continues until ended by the tenant serving notice to quit (for a periodic tenancy) or giving three months' notice (if his tenancy was for a fixed term), or the landlord can serve a notice in the prescribed form not less than 6 months or more than twelve months before the tenancy is to end.

If the tenant is unwilling to give up possession, he must serve a counter-notice to this effect (there is no prescribed form for this) within 2 months, and must apply to the court for a new tenancy within 2 to 4 months after the landlord's notice.

renewal

When the original tenancy comes to an end, provided that the landlord has not served a notice as above, the tenant may request a new tenancy (this right is only available to tenants who were originally granted a fixed term tenancy of more than 1 year). This is done by using a prescribed form. If the parties are not agreed as to the grant of a new tenancy, the tenant may apply to the court for one. He must make his application within 2 to 4 months of serving his notice requesting a new tenancy.

The time limits and procedures laid down in the Act have to be strictly observed. The various prescribed forms of notice are available from law stationers.

The court may grant a periodic or a fixed tenancy for a period of up to fourteen years. The court has wide discretion to decide the other provisions of the new agreement. The terms of the new lease will be largely governed by the terms of the old lease, unless either party can show that a variation should be made in the light of accepted commercial practice. If the court has to fix a rent, this will be an open market rent, disregarding such factors as any goodwill attaching to the premises because of the tenant's business there and any improvements made by the tenant (other than any made because of a contractual obligation to the landlord).

The landlord can oppose the tenant's request for a new tenancy on any of the grounds set out in section 30 of the Act. These apply in the same way as for assured tenancies, except that an offer of suitable accommodation must take into account the tenant's business needs. Thus the landlord must offer and be willing to provide suitable alternative accommodation on terms which are reasonable, having regard to the terms of the current tenancy and to all other relevant circumstances. These will include: whether the goodwill attaching to the premises will be preserved, the nature and character of the tenant's business and the situation, size and other facilities of the premises under the current tenancy. If the court is satisfied that the landlord has offered suitable alternative accommodation, it cannot grant a new tenancy (that is, it will refuse the tenant's application).

The original tenancy continues until the court hearing, and any notice ending it does not take effect until three months after the final hearing.

compensation for displacement

If the landlord successfully opposes the grant of a new tenancy where part only of the property is let on a sub-tenancy and the landlord wishes to let or sell it as a whole, or where he intends to reconstruct or demolish, or where he intends to occupy the premises for the purposes of his own business, compensation is payable when the tenant leaves. The amount is 3 times the rateable value of the premises. If for the past fourteen years the premises were occupied by the tenant or his predecessors in the same business, the compensation is doubled.

The parties may agree to exclude the compensation for displacement provisions, but only where the tenant has occupied the premises for the purpose of his business for less than five years.

compensation for improvements

Very generally speaking, an outgoing tenant is entitled to compensation for improvements he has made to the premises, other than any he was obliged to make under the terms of his tenancy agreement.

sub-letting

A mixed residential and business tenant may sub-let the whole or part of his premises, or assign his lease, unless the agreement does not allow him to do so. Usually the agreement will state that the consent of the landlord must first be obtained. In any lease which provides that the landlord's consent must be obtained to sub-letting or assignment, it is implied that such consent shall not be unreasonably withheld.

restricted contracts

A tenancy which is not within the scope of the Rent Acts, may be within the definition of what is called a 'restricted contract', and so may a licence agreement. Restricted contracts are subject to a lesser degree of statutory interference than other regulated tenancies, with a system of rent control but no security of tenure. There are a number of restraints on the landlord attempting to regain possession, but these were greatly reduced by the Housing Act 1980 for contracts made after 28 November 1980.

A restricted contract may be in writing or oral.

The statutory definition of a restricted contract gives little clue to its actual identity – '*a contract . . . whereby one person grants to another person, in consideration of a rent which includes payment for the use of furniture or for services, the right to occupy a dwelling as a residence*'. In practice, a restricted contract will arise if there is:

(i) *A tenancy where there is a resident landlord or where the tenant shares living accommodation with the landlord or others.* The requirement as to furniture or services does not need to be satisfied if there is a resident landlord. Nor does it have to be satisfied where, although the landlord is not resident, he (or some other person) does share living accommodation with the tenant – a kitchen or sitting room, for example. Both these types of tenancies are excluded from being regulated tenancies.

Lettings by resident landlords comprise the largest group of agreements within the restricted sector.

(ii) *A tenancy or a licence where the rent includes payment for furniture or services.* 'Services' is defined to include attendance (cleaning and laundry), the provision of heating or lighting, the supply of hot water and any other privilege or facility connected with the occupancy of a dwelling, other than access, cold water supply or w.c.

Most *tenancies* where furniture or services are provided are regulated tenancies fully protected under the Rent Act. The restricted contract net will catch those which are excluded from full Rent Act protection because, for instance, the rent includes a substantial payment for attendance, or the tenancy is a student letting by an educational establishment.

exclusive occupation
To be a restricted contract, the arrangement must give exclusive occupation, in return for a money payment. Exclusive occupation is implicit in tenancies that are restricted contracts: a tenancy cannot exist without it.

For a *licence* to be a restricted contract, not only must furniture or services be provided but the licensee must have exclusive occupation of at least one room that is his own, usually the bedroom. A hotel guest, a lodger or a paying guest may have a restricted contract, but it has been stressed by the courts that the accommodation must be more than of a temporary nature. The fact that a landlord had the right to enter 'at all times' will not prejudice the licensee's right to exclusive occupation.

Two persons can share a room as joint occupiers under a restricted contract. But if the licensee has to share his room with the landlord, or with someone chosen by the landlord, under a genuine non-exclusive occupation agreement, as would be the case in a hostel, then there is no exclusive occupation and no restricted contract. This was explained by Lord Goddard in a 1957 case. Mrs F had a contract as a so-called 'paying guest' to occupy an upper room in the P household. Lord Goddard said "The test is: had Mrs F the exclusive right to use the room as a residence? Mrs P, having let this room as a residence to Mrs F, had no right to come in and occupy it herself, nor had she a right to put somebody else into the room. I think that Mrs F had the exclusive right to use the room as a residence."

Usually service licences (for example, where live-in domestic staff have a room in the employer's house or flat) and family arrangements (for example, a girl's boyfriend staying in her parents' home) are not restricted contracts because rent is not paid.

DOES A RESTRICTED CONTRACT EXIST?

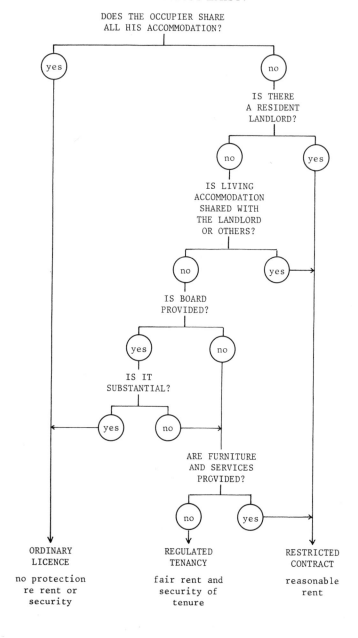

DOES THE OCCUPIER SHARE
ALL HIS ACCOMMODATION?

yes

no

IS THERE
A RESIDENT
LANDLORD?

no

yes

IS LIVING
ACCOMMODATION
SHARED WITH
THE LANDLORD
OR OTHERS?

no

yes

IS BOARD
PROVIDED?

yes

no

IS IT
SUBSTANTIAL?

yes

no

ARE FURNITURE
AND SERVICES
PROVIDED?

no

yes

ORDINARY
LICENCE

no protection
re rent or
security

REGULATED
TENANCY

fair rent and
security of
tenure

RESTRICTED
CONTRACT

reasonable
rent

In the following discussion, the word 'tenant' is used to describe the occupier under a restricted contract, be he tenant or licensee.

not a restricted contract
The basic definition of a restricted contract is qualified by excluding certain types of agreement. The agreement will not be a restricted contract where:

○ the rateable value of the occupier's part of the premises is more than £1,500 in Greater London and £750 elsewhere;
○ the rent includes a substantial payment for board (that is meals);
○ the landlord is the Crown, a government department or local authority, a registered housing association or a housing cooperative;
○ the letting is a regulated tenancy with full Rent Act protection;
○ the contract is to occupy a dwelling for a holiday.

The potential landlord will appreciate that the only way he can avoid the statutory provisions relating to regulated tenancies and restricted contracts is by:

○ granting a genuine non-exclusive occupation agreement
○ granting a genuine holiday letting
○ providing proper meals.

If there is any doubt whether there is a restricted contract, the matter will have to be resolved by the court.

rent control
If there is no registered rent for the premises, the rent is entirely a matter for agreement between the parties. But either the landlord or the tenant, or both of them together, or the local authority, may apply to the rent tribunal for a reasonable rent to be determined and registered (so the rent officer step is missed out: you go direct to the tribunal). The rent tribunal is the rent assessment committee in another guise. Its composition is the same, namely a layman, a surveyor and a lawyer-chairman.

An application to the rent tribunal is made on a standard prescribed form, FR2, available from the clerk to the tribunal. The names and addresses of the landlord and tenant must be given together with the address of the premises, details of the accommodation and any furniture and services provided, the rent payable and any meals supplied. A copy of any written agreement should accompany the form.

Provided that an application has not been withdrawn 'before the tribunal have entered upon consideration of it' (which apparently means before all the panel members have started to read the papers), they must consider it, make the appropriate enquiries (which often includes a visit to the premises) and either arrange a hearing or ask for written representations from the parties. If a hearing is called, it is fairly informal and will follow much the same format as a hearing before the rent assessment committee. To help it make a decision, the rent tribunal may ask the landlord to furnish it with certain information. Wilful refusal on the part of a landlord so to do is a criminal offence.

If there is any doubt whether there is a restricted contract, a resolution of the court under section 141 of the Rent Act will have to be sought.

'reasonable rent'

The reasonable rent which the tribunal arrives at may be higher, or lower, or the same as the existing one. Unlike the assessment of a fair rent, there is no statutory provision about factors the tribunal much take into account (age, state and condition of the premises and so on) or disregard (scarcity value, for example). Reasonable rents may therefore be higher than fair rents but lower than market rents. The tribunal notifies its decision to the parties in writing but is not bound to give reasons for it, unless specifically asked to do so. There is no appeal from a tribunal decision except to the High Court on a point of law or matter of natural justice.

All reasonable rents are entered on a register maintained by the tribunal. This is open to public inspection, so anyone who is intending to let or rent accommodation under a restricted contract can see what a reasonable rent is likely to be.

Where a reasonable rent is registered, this is the maximum rent the landlord can charge until it is cancelled (so it continues to apply to a new tenant). He commits a criminal offence if he charges more. Any excess rent the tenant has paid is recoverable from the landlord. Apart from a liability to repay the offending payment to the tenant, on court order, the landlord is liable to a fine or up to 6 months' imprisonment (or both). So if necessary, the tenant can take county court proceedings to get back the overpayment.

If the registered rent is higher than the previous one, the tenant must pay it immediately. The increase is not subject to phasing.

A reasonable rent does not include rates. If the landlord pays rates for the accommodation, he can recover these (and any increase in rates) from the tenant, in addition to the reasonable rent.

cancellation
An application for the cancellation of a registered rent may be made to the rent tribunal if the following conditions are satisfied:

(i) the registration is at least 2 years old; *and*
(ii) the accommodation is not currently subject to a restricted contract (for example because it is empty); *and*
(iii) the application is made by the person who would, but for (ii), be the landlord.

The application for cancellation must be made on a special form, obtainable from the clerk to the tribunal. The cancellation of a registered rent does not prejudice any future application for the registration of a reasonable rent, if there is a new letting.

In addition, either the landlord, or the tenant, or both together, or the local authority may apply to the tribunal to review or reconsider the rent, provided that two years or more have elapsed since the date they considered it last. Such an application may then be made at any time where

○ the landlord and tenant apply jointly; or
○ there is a change in the condition of the accommodation, the furniture or services supplied, the terms of the contract or any other circumstances accounted for in the tribunal's previous decision.

Application has to be made on a standard form.

no premiums
If a reasonable rent is registered for the premises (but not otherwise) it is illegal to charge a premium for the grant or assignment of a

restricted contract. The landlord may take a deposit from the tenant against non-payment of bills or damage to furniture and so on, but this must not be more than two months' rent.

rent books
Where rent is payable weekly under a restricted contract, the landlord has to provide a rent book, containing certain notices and particulars of rent and of the other terms and conditions of the contract.

terminating a restricted contract

If the tenant entered into a restricted contract after 28 November 1980, he has no security of tenure. If he has a *periodic tenancy*, the landlord must give at least four weeks' notice in the prescribed form (in writing, containing certain prescribed information). In the case of a *fixed term tenancy*, no notice to quit is normally required: the tenancy will come to an end when the fixed term expires. The same is true of a licence. However, where the terms of the agreement provide for a notice to quit to be given, the landlord will have to comply.

Irrespective of whether the contract amounts to a tenancy or a licence, there can be no eviction without a court order for possession. When the notice to quit expires, or at the end of the fixed term or licence, the landlord must go to the court if the tenant or licensee does not leave. Proceedings are taken in the county court and, although possession cannot be refused, the court has the power to postpone the date on which it must be given. The postponement cannot be for longer than 3 months. When possession is postponed, the court will impose conditions on the tenant regarding the payment of current rent and any arrears (unless exceptional hardship would be caused to the tenant, or it is otherwise unreasonable). If the tenant breaks these conditions or otherwise misbehaves (uses the accommodation for immoral purposes, for instance) the landlord may ask the court for an earlier date for possession. But to prevent an unlawful eviction, the landlord needs to obtain a warrant for possession.

pre-November 1980 restricted contracts

If the contract was entered into before 28 November 1980, the tenant still has no security of tenure but is in a better position because of the greater delaying devices available to him. With pre-1980 contracts, a distinction has to be drawn between contracts which are determinable by notice to quit and those which are not.

The following rules apply only where a valid notice to quit has been served (for periodic tenancies, this is at least 4 weeks notice in the prescribed form; for fixed term tenancies and licences which require notices to quit, it has to be a notice which complies with the terms of the agreement and allows a reasonable time for the quitting of the premises).

(i) If a notice to quit is served *by the landlord* after the tenant has applied to the rent tribunal for a reasonable rent to be assessed, the notice is automatically suspended until six months after the rent tribunal's decision. (This period can be reduced by the tribunal.) When the period has expired, the tenant may apply for a further postponement under a different section (see ii below) of the Act. There is no limit to the number of postponements that can be applied for.

(ii) Where a notice to quit has been served by *either party* and the contract has been referred to the rent tribunal for the determination of a reasonable rent (before or after the notice to quit has been served), the tenant may apply to the tribunal for a postponement of the notice. But he must do so before the notice expires. The notice is then postponed until the tribunal reaches its decision as to the rent, and the tribunal may, as part of its decision, suspend the operation of the notice for up to six months from the date on which it would otherwise have expired – that is, for example, at the end of an extension under (i) above, or a previous postponement under this (ii) paragraph. The tribunal is not bound to exercise this discretion and, if it refuses to do so, the notice is postponed for 7 days after the tribunal's decision and the tenant cannot apply for a further extension.

If the tenant breaks the terms of the contract or otherwise misbehaves (causes a nuisance to neighbours, for instance) during any period of suspension, the landlord can go back to the tribunal and ask them to bring forward the date for possession.

These rules depend on a valid notice to quit having been served, so they apply in the main to periodic tenancies only. Fixed term tenants and licensees (whose agreements provide that occupation shall cease on a certain date) have no right to remain when their term ends.

If a landlord granted a fixed-term tenancy to an existing tenant, before 28 November 1980 (that is, a second tenancy which was for a fixed term), the tenant will be a fully protected tenant under the Rent Act and therefore entitled to remain in possession after the end of the fixed term.

The Department of the Environment's booklet *Letting Rooms in Your Home* (a guide for resident landlords and their tenants) includes a section on the special rules which apply to lettings that began before 28 November 1980.

special note for resident landlords

If a landlord ceases to be a resident landlord on a permanent basis, the restricted contract tenancy becomes a regulated tenancy under the Rent Act. However, in the following two situations the letting will remain a restricted contract even where the landlord is not resident:

○ If the premises are sold and the buyer (the new landlord) gives the tenant notice within 28 days that he intends to take up residence and does so within six months.

○ If a resident landlord has died, two years are allowed for the winding-up of the estate. During this period, a person who has inherited the dwelling may move into residence, or the personal representatives of the deceased landlord may exercise the rights of a resident landlord to obtain possession. If the property is owned by joint tenants and the survivor does not live there (although for this exception to operate at all, one of the joint owners must have lived at the property) it will be that person, the survivor, who is entitled to obtain vacant possession of the property, by serving the appropriate notice and obtaining the court order for possession.

long tenancies at low rents

The Rent Act 1977 does not cover residential tenants with a long lease at a low rent. The basic protection given to residential occupiers by the Protection from Eviction Act applies, however, and the Landlord and Tenant Act 1954 and the Leasehold Reform Act 1967 give them valuable rights, both during and at the end of the tenancy.

the Landlord and Tenant Act 1954

Part I of the Landlord and Tenant Act 1954 applies to residential tenants who have a long lease and pay a low rent. It is particularly important to such tenants of flats, because they cannot take advantage of the provisions of the Leasehold Reform Act 1967 (which applies to long leases of houses only, not flats) and would otherwise have no protection.

A long lease is one which is granted for a term of over 21 years and which cannot be ended prematurely by a landlord's notice. A low rent is one that is less than $\frac{2}{3}$ of the rateable value of the property. Sums payable for maintenance, services, insurance and rates are disregarded from the calculation, and the appropriate rateable value for this purpose is the rateable value on 23 March 1965 or when first rated, if later. The tenancy must be one which, apart from its low rent, would otherwise be within the Rent Act. Basically, there must be a letting of accommodation which the tenant occupies as his home, within certain rateable value limits.

security of tenure

During the fixed term, the landlord can regain possession only pursuant to a forfeiture clause if the tenant breaks the terms of his tenancy agreement and then only by going through the courts. When the fixed term runs out, the tenancy continues on the same terms until ended by the landlord or the tenant in the proper manner.

A tenant can terminate the tenancy by giving one month's notice. He can serve this early, so that the notice expires on the original term date. A landlord must serve not less than 6 months' nor more than 12 months' notice on the tenant. His notice must include either

○ proposals for a new statutory tenancy specifying the accommodation, the rent and other terms of the agreement; or

○ a warning that if the tenant is not willing to give up possession, the landlord will apply to the court for possession on stated grounds.

The parties should agree to the terms of the statutory tenancy or apply to the court to settle the matter within two months, otherwise the notice lapses. When the terms have been decided, the tenant has an ordinary statutory tenancy under the Rent Act 1977. All the grounds for possession apply and either party may ask for the registration of a fair rent.

Alternatively, if the landlord wants possession, grounds on which he can seek possession are

○ that the tenant has not paid the rent, or has broken some other term of the tenancy

○ that the tenant or a person living with him has caused a nuisance or annoyance to neighbours or has been convicted of immoral or illegal use of the premises

○ that the landlord requires the property for his family or himself

○ that the landlord has offered suitable alternative accommodation.

These grounds are discretionary: the court may grant an order for possession if it thinks it reasonable to do so. If the order is refused, the tenancy continues on the same terms are before.

the Leasehold Reform Act 1967

The Leasehold Reform Act 1967 as amended by the Leasehold Reform Act 1979 and the Housing Act 1980, gives valuable rights to tenants in the private and public sector who are occupying a house under a long lease at a low rent (commonly called a ground rent). The leases were often 'building' leases at a very low ground rent for terms of 99 or 125 years. The tenant therefore built and maintained a house which at the end of the term became the landlord's entitlement. The problem became great in the 1960's when many such leases expired.

The purpose of the Act is to allow the tenant

○ to buy the freehold (the tenant's right to enfranchise); or
○ to extend the period of the lease for up to 50 years; or
○ to remain in occupation of the property when the lease expires, as a statutory tenant.

A tenant who wishes to buy the freehold or extend the lease must give the landlord notice of this intention before the original term granted by the lease expires.

The tenant must be an individual (companies and businesses are excluded) and meet all the following conditions:

i he must have a lease of a house; *and*
ii the lease must be for a long term; *and*
iii the rent must be a low rent; *and*
iv the rateable value of the house must fall within prescribed limits; *and*
v he must have occupied the house as his only or main residence for the whole of the last three years, or for a total of three out of the last ten years.

a house

Most detached, semi-detached and terraced houses satisfy the 'house' condition. The Act does not contain an exhaustive definition of the word, but lays down certain broad rules.

○ The fact that a building is not structurally detached does not prevent it from being a house.

○ An individual maisonette or flat cannot be a house, but the whole building can be, even though it is divided horizontally into maisonettes or flats. So, if a tenant of a large house divides it into flats, lets the upper floors and lives in the ground floor flat himself, he will be able to buy the freehold or extend his lease of the house, but his tenants cannot.

○ If the building is divided vertically into units, it is not a house, but the individual units may be. Thus, leases of semi-detached or terraced houses may be individually enfranchised or extended.

When accommodation is used for mixed residential and business purposes and cannot be divided into separate vertical units, as long as such accommodation can reasonably be called a house, it will come under the Act, provided it satisfies the other conditions.

a long lease
A long lease is normally one which has been granted for a term of more than twenty-one years. However, a lease for less than 21 years acquired under the right to buy provisions contained in the Housing Act 1985 is treated as a long lease for these purposes. The tenant does not have to be the original tenant, he may be an assignee (that is, someone who has bought the lease).

Where the tenant's term of the lease was originally for less than 21 years but has been renewed, he may have a long lease if the original and renewed terms together add up to more than 21 years. No premium (lump sum) must have been paid for the renewal and there must have been an obligation on the part of the landlord to renew, contained in the original lease.

Landlords used to be able to avoid the Act by granting a lease terminable by notice after any death or marriage. This loophole was narrowed by the Housing Act 1980 for leases granted after 18 April 1980. Now such a provision can help the landlord only if

○ the notice can only be served within three months after the tenant's death or marriage (nobody else's)
   and

○ the lease contains an absolute prohibition on selling or sub-letting the whole of the property.

a low rent

The annual rent must be less than two-thirds of the rateable value of the house assessed on 23 March 1965, or the date on which the property first appeared in the valuation list, or the first day of the term granted by the lease, whichever is the later. The local authority's valuation officer will help with enquiries relating to rateable values.

A lease will be outside the Act if it was granted between 31 August 1939 and 1 April 1963 and the rent at the beginning of the tenancy was more than two-thirds of the letting value of the property. The 'letting value' of a property is the amount which could be obtained by a landlord letting on the open market.

Any amounts paid by a tenant towards the landlord's costs of insuring the building, providing services or carrying out repairs are disregarded in calculating 'low rents', irrespective of when the lease was created.

Rent payable under a shared ownership lease acquired under the Housing Act 1985 is not a low rent for these purposes if it is in excess of £10 per annum. (Shared ownership is dealt with later in this book.)

rateable values

The relevant date, known as 'the appropriate day', on which the rateable value is taken is 23 March 1965, or if later, the date when the property first appeared in the valuation list for rating purposes.

Here is a table of the limits, if the tenancy was granted:

	on or before *18 February 1966*	*on or after* *19 February 1966*
Greater *London*	(a) £400; or (b) £1,500 if the	(a) £400; or (b) £1,000 if the
	property appears in the valuation list for the first time after 1 April 1973	
Elsewhere	(a) £200; or (b) £750 if the	(a) £200; or (b) £500 if the
	property appears in the valuation list for the first time after 1 April 1973	

Note

If the 'appropriate date' was before 1 April 1973 and the rateable value was more than £400 (in Greater London) or £200 (elsewhere), then 1 April 1973 is substituted as 'the appropriate day' and provided the rateable value was not more than £1,500 (in Greater London) or £750 (elsewhere) on that date, the property will be within the prescribed limits. The provision does not apply to tenancies granted on or after 19 February 1966.

The rateable value of some properties was re-assessed to take effect from 1 April 1973. If the rateable value was increased because of improvements made by the tenant or his predecessors, the tenant may be entitled to a notional reduction for the purpose of bringing the house within the rateable value limits (but not for assessing rates payable). A tenant who is entitled to a notional reduction should inform his landlord by notice in writing (there is a prescribed form for this, which requires details of the improvements and who paid for them) and ask the landlord to agree a figure for the reduction, within six weeks. If no agreement is reached, the tenant may apply (between six and twelve weeks after service of the notice) to the county court for it to decide the reduction. The court office will inform the tenant how to make an application.

three years' occupation
If a tenant occupies a house for two years by virtue of a monthly tenancy and then takes a long lease of the house at a low rent, the first two years of occupation cannot be used to fulfil the three-year condition: he must wait until three years have elapsed from the date he took the long lease.

If the tenant inherited the lease, any period of occupation by a member of his family who was the previous tenant can count towards the three year period, provided the tenant was during that time also living in the house. 'Member of the family' means husband or wife, son, daughter (including adopted children, step-children and illegitimate children), son-in-law or daughter-in-law of the tenant or of the tenant's wife or husband, and the father or mother of the tenant or tenant's wife or husband.

The tenant need not live in the whole of the house. He still comes within the Act if he lets off part, provided he has occupied that or some other part as his only or main residence for the whole of the last three years or a total of three years during the last ten.

the right to buy the freehold

A tenant has the right to buy only that which was the subject matter of a lease covered by the Act. He cannot compel the landlord to sell him a garden, garage or outbuilding which he has been using unless it was also included in the lease of the house, nor has he a right to buy a garage or garden let to him under a totally different lease. It is perfectly permissible, however, for the tenant to agree to buy these separately from a landlord. (They will probably be of little use to the landlord or anyone else.)

A landlord may suffer hardship if he is forced to sell his house to a tenant, while himself retaining another part of the same building. For example, the landlord may have the use of one small room in a building, the rest of which is the tenant's house. To sell the house to the tenant may well render that small room valueless. Where this is the case, the landlord may, within two months of receiving notice that his tenant wishes to enfranchise, serve a notice on the tenant objecting to the severance of the house from the rest of the building (in our example, the small room) and asking the tenant to buy it along with the house. If the tenant does not object, a price for the remainder of the building has to be agreed. The landlord can ask any price he wants for that small room. If agreement cannot be reached, the matter will ultimately have to be referred to the county court to decide whether it is reasonable for the tenant to buy the part of the building specified in the landlord's notice.

A similar procedure exists when a landlord wishes to reduce the extent of the premises he is statutorily bound to sell to his tenant. Again, if the landlord and tenant cannot agree about the reduction, the matter can be referred to the county court. In deciding, the court will have regard to any hardship which would be caused to the tenant if it grants the reduction of the premises (and vice versa).

Legal ownership of a house does not merely mean owning bricks and mortar. It includes a bundle of legal rights necessary for the proper enjoyment of the house, for example to use pipes and cables crossing a neighbour's land for the supply of electricity, water and other services, and to use a private road running along the back of the house. A tenant will normally be expressly granted such rights in his lease.

The Act ensures that when the tenant buys the freehold, he will enjoy similar rights. In so far as the landlord is able, he must grant to his buyer-tenant such rights as are necessary to ensure that the buyer's position is the same as when he was a tenant.

The Act also ensures that the landlord and neighbours retain any rights that they enjoyed before the tenant enfranchised. When the landlord sells the freehold interest in the house, he may insist on retaining some of the rights which he (or some other person) enjoyed over part of the buyer-tenant's house when it was held under the long lease.

the price

The policy behind the Leasehold Reform Act is to treat the tenant as the owner of the building and the landlord merely as the owner of the land on which the house stands. The tenant is, accordingly, able to buy the freehold at a favourable price.

The price payable will be the open market value of the freehold in the house subject to one of two sets of assumptions laid down by the Act, based on the rateable value of the house on the date the tenant gives the landlord notice of his intention to buy the freehold.

If the rateable value is £1,000 or less in Greater London, or £500 or less elsewhere, the assumptions are that

○ the landlord is selling the freehold subject to the tenancy and the tenancy has been extended under the Act
○ the landlord is willing to sell but the tenant does not have the right to compel him to sell
○ the sale is subject to and with the benefits of the existing rights, and subject to the existing incumbrances affecting the property (provided that these will bind the tenant once the sale is completed)
○ any defect in the title of the landlord would result in a discount in accordance with the principle applicable to sales on the open market
○ the tenant does not have any special interest in buying the landlord's reversionary interest.

If the rateable value in Greater London is between £1,001 and £1,500, and elsewhere is between £501 and £750, the assumptions are that

○ the landlord is selling the freehold subject to the tenancy
○ at the end of the tenancy, the tenant will have the right to remain in occupation under the provisions of Part I of the Landlord and Tenant Act 1954
○ the tenant has no liability to carry out repairs either under the terms of the lease or the provisions of Part I of the Landlord and Tenant Act 1954
○ the value of the house has not been increased by any improvements made by the tenant
○ the sale is subject to and with the benefit of the rights and subject to existing incumbrances affecting the enjoyment of the property (provided that these will bind the tenant once the sale is completed).

The principal difference between the two bases is that in the first (where the rateable value is lower) the increased value of the landlord's reversion (the freehold) to the tenant is ignored, as if a third party were buying. If the property were sold to a third party, it would be sold subject to the long lease without vacant possession and the price would have to be discounted to take account of this fact. If, however, the tenant, rather than a third party, buys the freehold, his leasehold interest disappears and he then has a freehold which is not subject to any sort of lease. In other words, the freehold is much more valuable to the tenant than to a third party buyer.

disputes as to the price
A landlord or a tenant may ask the local leasehold valuation tribunal (the address is the same as for the rent assessment committee and can be found in the telephone directory) to determine the price to be paid by a tenant who wishes to buy the freehold under the Act. A tenant may apply as soon as the landlord has named a price or after two months from the date he served his notice of intention to buy. Application is made on form 1, obtainable from the law stationers or the tribunal's offices.

The leasehold valuation tribunal is made up of three people drawn from the rent assessment panel for the area. One member must be a qualified valuer. There is no fee for applying to the tribunal.

A hearing date is set by the tribunal. At the hearing, both parties are given the opportunity to state their case, calling such witnesses as they feel necessary. The proceedings tend to be informal. Shortly after the hearing, each party to the application is sent a document by the tribunal, stating the price (and such other decisions as may be relevant) and the reasons for their decision.

Either party may appeal to the lands tribunal against a decision by the leasehold valuation tribunal. Appeal must be made within 28 days of the latter's decision. A fee is payable and the unsuccessful party may have to pay, or contribute towards, the other's costs.

covenants, where a tenant enfranchises

A lease usually contains a variety of covenants which impose obligations on both the landlord and the tenant in relation to matters such as the payment of rent and rates, insurance, repairs and use of the property. When a tenant enfranchises and becomes the freehold owner, most of the covenants become inappropriate, and therefore disappear. However, the tenant will be bound by interests which were already attached to the freehold (such as rights of way and restrictive covenants), and will remain bound by sub-tenancies, mortgages etc created out of his own tenancy.

The Leasehold Reform Act also provides that in some circumstances the conveyance of the freehold to the tenant may be subject to further obligations, as follows.

'schemes of management'
Where an estate is controlled by a single landlord, each tenant is normally subject to a series of obligations, designed to ensure that the general appearance of the estate is suitably maintained. Since these obligations would otherwise disappear on enfranchisement (and the estate would suffer as a result) the landlord can apply to the

High Court to have a 'scheme of management' approved, which means that he will have power to:

○ carry out work for the maintenance or repair of any property which was formerly leasehold but which has been bought by a tenant;
○ regulate development of, and impose restrictions on, the use of such properties;
○ require a tenant who has bought the freehold under the Act to contribute towards the maintenance and repair of the property where the (ex-)landlord has incurred expense for this purpose under the scheme.

The existence of such a scheme can be discovered by a 'search' of the local land charges register. A local land charges search is made at the offices of the local district council (or, in London, the appropriate borough council) on form LLC1. The register of local land charges is divided into twelve parts and it is worth applying for a search of the whole register rather than to confine oneself to this single issue. The cost is £3.10. (It takes a few weeks for a local land charges search to be processed. To save time, it may be made in person.) If the search reveals that the property is subject to a scheme of management (the search certificate would show it as a registered charge), the enfranchising tenant should write to the local authority to ask for details of the landlord's powers. The search itself only indicates the existence of the scheme; a letter would elicit further details from the local authority. As long as the landlord's powers are not unduly onerous, the tenant is likely to benefit from the scheme, as it will mean that the standard of the estate can be adequately maintained.

When carrying out the local search just mentioned, the tenant should also submit a form of enquiries to the local authority on form Con.29A (or, in London, Con.29D) which will reveal other information about the property – for example, whether there are any proposals to build new roads in the area, where the drains are, and so on. It may be that on the basis of the information which the tenant receives from the authority, he may decide not to proceed at all. The combined cost of a local land charges search and the making of such enquiries is £14.40. The whole subject of local searches and enquiries of local authorities is dealt with in detail in its context in the Consumer Publication *The legal side of buying a house*.

reservation of rights to develop

Where the tenant is enfranchising from certain public sector land-lords, such as a local authority or a new town development corporation, covenants may be imposed on the tenant restricting the carrying out of developments or clearing of land, where this is necessary to preserve the land for possible development by the original landlord.

rights to pre-emption

In some cases where the freehold is acquired from particular landlords such as the Commission for the New Towns, the landlord may insert in the conveyance to the enfranchising tenant a term that the house should not be resold without the landlord's consent, and that the landlord shall have the right to buy back the property in the event of any proposal to sell it. This is called a right of pre-emption, namely a right of refusal in respect of a piece of land before the opportunity to purchase it is offered to others.

mortgages

A landlord may have mortgaged his interest in the property – perhaps to enable him to buy it in the first place. What happens to such a mortgage if the tenant acquires the freehold? The answer is that the tenant will take the property free from the mortgage, provided that he pays the purchase price to the mortgagee (the lender) rather than to the freehold owner. (If there is more than one mortgage to be paid off, they must be paid off in order of priority, broadly speaking according to the date on which they were created. In cases of doubt, a solicitor should be consulted.)

It is extremely important for a tenant first to find out if his landlord (or anyone else with a superior interest) has a mortgage, and to ensure that the purchase price is paid to that mortgagee. If the tenant does not pay the purchase price to his landlord's mortgagee, the property he buys will remain subject to the mortgage to the extent of the purchase price.

It is not necessary for the landlord to obtain the mortgagee's consent to the sale, nor for a mortgagee to be joined as a party to the conveyance or transfer.

The fact that the house and premises are released from the mortgage does not necessarily mean that the mortgage will be completely paid off. If the purchase price is not sufficient to pay off the total amount of the landlord's indebtedness to the mortgagee, the landlord will still remain personally liable to pay off the balance (and can be sued for it).

If the tenant cannot discover whether the landlord has mortgaged his interest, or the identity of a mortgagee, he should pay the purchase price into court. The same is true if a mortgagee proves to be unhelpful and, for example, refuses to sign a release of the house from the mortgage. The county court office will tell the tenant how to do this.

the right to extend the lease

The tenant who cannot afford to buy the freehold or does not wish to do so, may choose to claim an extension of his existing lease. Once a tenant gives notice to his landlord that he wishes to claim an extension, the landlord has to grant him a new tenancy in substitution for the existing one.

The terms of that new lease will be as follows:

1 *Duration:* The landlord has to grant an extension of fifty years. The new lease will expire 50 years after the date on which, but for the Act, the existing lease would have expired.

2 *Property included in the new lease:* Broadly speaking, the premises comprised in the new lease will be the same as those contained in the tenant's existing lease. However, similar to the situation when a tenant exercises his right to buy the freehold, the landlord may increase or reduce the premises to be included in the new lease.

3 *Rent:* The tenant continues to pay the agreed rent until the date on which his existing lease expires. Thereafter, he has to pay a new 'ground rent', based on the letting value of the land on which the house stands (ignoring any value attributable to the house or other buildings). The use to which the land may be put will be taken into consideration. Thus if the site is ripe for redevelopment, the rent will reflect this and be higher.

The landlord can require the new ground rent to be reviewed after twenty-five years; he has to serve notice on the tenant during the twenty-fourth year of the new lease. The reviewed ground rent is calculated in the same way as the new ground rent was.

The leasehold valuation tribunal has the power to fix a new ground rent, on the application of either the landlord or the tenant. Application is made on form 2 (*Application for determination by leasehold valuation tribunal of the rent to be payable*), which contains 13 questions most of which are self-explanatory.

The amount of the new ground rent (and any reviewed rent) must not be assessed until the year before the tenant's existing lease is to expire (or the twenty-fourth year of the extended period). This is to ensure that in a fluctuating property market a fair rent is arrived at.

Any payment towards services which the landlord has to provide under the terms of the new tenancy will be in addition to the new ground rent. If the tenant's existing lease requires him to contribute a fixed sum towards services and over the course of time this figure has become unrealistic, the Act says that 'such provision as may be just' should be made for payments by the tenant. Failing agreement between the parties, the leasehold valuation tribunal may be asked to fix a figure.

4   *Other terms:*   As a general rule, the provisions of the new lease will be the same as those in the tenant's existing lease (although they can be varied by agreement). There are some important exceptions to this:

(i) Where the property to be included in the new lease is not exactly the same as that in the original one, the new lease may contain any necessary modifications. For instance, if the landlord has reduced the premises originally let to the tenant, his repair obligations under the new lease will be less extensive.

(ii) It is not possible to include in the new lease a right of renewal of the lease, a right of pre-emption (that is a right of first refusal if the landlord decides to sell) or an option to purchase the freehold. A tenant should think carefully whether he wishes to lose these valuable rights.

(iii) The new lease will not contain a provision which allows the landlord to terminate the tenancy prematurely, otherwise than in the event of breach of covenant by the tenant.

(iv) The new lease must contain a provision that no long sub-tenancy can confer on a new sub-tenant any right to buy the freehold or extend the sub-tenancy under the Act.

(v) The new lease must provide that the landlord has the right to resume possession of the property for the purposes of redeveloping it. Section 17 gives the landlord the right to seek possession from the court at any time, if he can prove that for the purposes of redevelopment he proposes to demolish or reconstruct the whole or a substantial part of the property.

A landlord who successfully obtains possession against a tenant under this provision, will have to pay the tenant compensation. The amount of compensation is what the house would be expected to realise in the open market if sold by a willing seller on certain assumptions – such as that the property is vacant and subject to existing incumbrances and restrictions and not subject to a tenant's right to buy the freehold.

If the parties cannot agree a figure for compensation, either can apply to the leasehold valuation tribunal for the matter to be settled. Application is made on Form 3 (*Application for determination by leasehold valuation tribunal of compensation payable to a tenant*).

tenant loses right to buy the freehold

When a tenant claims an extension of his lease under the Act, he retains his right to buy the freehold, but only until the date on which his original lease expires. So, if he does not serve the landlord with notice of his intention to buy the freehold before that date, he will have to give up possession at the end of his extended 50 years lease. He has no right to a further extension under the Act and is not protected by the Rent Act 1977 when the extended lease expires, so that he will not benefit from security of tenure or be able to have a fair rent registered.

A tenant should remember that his lease will almost certainly contain a covenant by him to repair the property. At the end of his lease he will be required to ensure that the property is in a good state of repair. The landlord may serve a schedule of dilapidations setting out the work he feels necessary to put the premises in proper order. If a tenant has failed to meet his repair obligations during the tenancy, he may have to pay for the repairs in one lump sum.

the tenant's right to stay on

A tenant may choose not to exercise his right to buy the freehold or claim an extended lease, or perhaps he will not have occupied the property for the qualifying period of three years before the long lease expires. In these circumstances, provided that the property is within the current rateable value limits laid down by the Rent Act, the tenant has the right to remain in possession of the property as a statutory tenant.

Briefly, a statutory tenant has the right to remain in possession and on his death a member of his family may succeed to the statutory tenancy. A statutory tenant may apply to have a fair rent registered for the property.

opposing a tenant's claim to enfranchise or to an extended lease

If the conditions laid down by the Act are not satisfied, the tenant cannot claim any of the rights conferred by it.

A landlord may oppose a claim by his tenant to buy the freehold or extend the lease on one of several grounds.

1   landlord requires the property for his own occupation

The landlord may apply to the county court for possession of the house when the original lease expires. He must apply during the term of the original lease but after the tenant has served notice claiming his rights under the Act. The court office will help with applications.

To oppose the tenant's claim successfully the landlord must show

○ that he acquired his interest in the house before 19 February 1966
○ that the house or part of it is, or will be, reasonably required by him, or an adult (over 18) member of his family, as his or their only or main residence on the date the tenant's original lease expires. For this purpose, member of a landlord's family means

spouse, son or daughter, son- or daughter-in-law, father or mother, father- or mother-in-law; adopted, illegitimate and step-children qualify.
○ that it would cause greater hardship to him or the member of the family if the court did not make an order for possession than would be the case if the tenant had to give up possession at the end of the lease. The landlord must produce sufficient evidence of the hardship.

The court has absolute discretion as to the granting of such orders. If the landlord is successful, the court will make an order specifying a date when he can re-take possession. The tenant will be entitled to compensation for his loss of the house and premises, the amount of which is assessed as if a landlord re-takes possession for the purposes of redevelopment.

A landlord who makes an unsuccessful application to the court on the ground of needing the property for his own occupation, may submit another application if his circumstances change.

2 redevelopment

A landlord whose tenant has claimed an extended lease may regain possession if he intends to demolish or reconstruct the whole or a substantial part of the premises for the purposes of redevelopment. Compensation is payable to the outgoing tenant.

The Act contains special provisions applicable to landlords which are public authorities such as county and district councils, universities, nationalised industries, health authorities and so on. If a public authority obtains a certificate from the appropriate minister (usually the Secretary for State for the Environment) stating that it will need the property for development within the next ten years, that public authority will be able to resist a tenant's claim to buy the freehold or extend the lease. Again, a tenant whose rights under the Act are taken away in this manner is entitled to compensation.

3 where the Crown has an interest

Generally speaking, the Crown is not bound by the provisions of the Act and the tenant may find that he is unable to take advantage of the Act. Tenants, for example, of the Crown Lands Commissioners, a government department or the Duchy of Cornwall may find themselves in this position.

In practice, however, the Crown usually allows a tenant to exercise his right to enfranchise or extend his lease, unless the property is of special architectural or historic interest or is needed for development or some public purposes.

If the Crown is not the tenant's immediate landlord and the tenant is only claiming an extended lease, provided that the immediate landlord has at least fifty years' leasehold interest in the property, the tenant can proceed in the normal way and the Crown's interest can then generally be ignored.

4 tenant has previously given a notice to quit

If the landlord can prove that a tenant's notice claiming to acquire the freehold or an extended lease is made after a tenant has given notice to quit, the claim is invalid.

The Act provides that if a tenant makes a claim under the Act towards the end of his original lease, the tenancy is not to expire and cannot be terminated by a landlord serving notice to quit. The lease is extended for so long as the claim by the tenant is being dealt with, plus a further three months of grace afterwards.

special provisions relating to sub-tenants

The fact that the tenant in occupation is a sub-tenant (or a sub-subtenant) does not prevent him from buying the freehold, claiming an extended lease, or staying on as a statutory tenant, provided all the conditions for the application of the Act are otherwise fulfilled. The Act makes special provision to enable all the superior interests (that is the interest of the tenant in occupation's landlord and other interests higher up the chain) to be dealt with.

the reversioner

To simplify the procedure, the Act states that the tenant shall deal with one person only – 'the reversioner' (although everyone with an interest in the property will be notified of the proceedings). The reversioner has the power to conduct the proceedings, once a sub-tenant has given notice claiming his statutory rights. He can execute a conveyance of the freehold to the sub-tenant or grant a new extended lease, and he binds any landlords with interests superior to the tenant in occupation. Furthermore, the reversioner is entitled to call upon all landlords with superior interests to produce documents in order to ensure that the tenant gets good title.

The reversioner may be:

(a) the first landlord higher up the chain of tenancies from the tenant in occupation who (on expiry of the tenant's lease) would have an expectation of at least thirty years' possession of the property. So, if the tenant's immediate landlord only has a reversionary interest of two years (that is, his lease expires two years after the tenant's) the tenant must move up the chain to the next landlord until he finds one who has a reversion of at least thirty years; or

(b) if nobody qualifies in paragraph (a) the reversioner is the owner of the freehold interest.

However, the notice a sub-tenant has to give under the Act must be served on his immediate landlord. The sub-tenant should also serve the notice on any other superior landlord of whom he knows.

price

The existence of superior interests does not mean that a tenant buying the freehold has to pay more for it. He simply buys out the interests of each superior landlord separately. These interests are valued on the basis of what they would fetch in a sale on the open market. Clearly the longer the reversion of a superior landlord, the more it is worth. But the sum total paid by the tenant should not normally exceed the amount he would have to pay if his landlord was the freeholder.

In one case the Act lays down a formula for calculating the price to be paid to a superior landlord; this is where the superior landlord's lease would expire within one month of the date of the occupying tenant's lease and the superior landlord's profit rent is not more than £5 per year. Profit rent is calculated by subtracting the rent paid to the superior landlord by his tenant from the rent paid by that superior landlord to his own landlord.

procedure

The Leasehold Reform Act lays down the procedure that must be followed by a landlord and tenant when a claim is made.

the tenant's notice

It is wise for the tenant to keep copies of any notices he sends, for future reference. A tenant must give the landlord notice of his intention to buy the freehold or claim an extended lease on form 1 *'Notice of leaseholder's claim'*. (If the notice is served by a sub-tenant, he should serve it on his own landlord and on anyone with a superior interest of whom he knows.) If the tenant is buying the freehold and knows that his landlord has a mortgage on the property, a copy of the notice should be served on the mortgagee.

Form 1 comprises 8 paragraphs, a schedule and 8 notes (referred to in the margin of the form).

In paragraph 1, the tenant must delete one of the two alternatives namely 'freehold' or 'extended lease'. A notice which does not state clearly which alternative the tenant is opting for will be invalid.

Paragraph 2 should be modified by the tenant by deleting one of the alternatives which appear in square brackets.

If a tenant knows that his landlord is the owner of the freehold, he may delete paragraphs 3 to 8 which apply only to claims by sub-tenants, and move on to complete the schedule.

The schedule to form 1 *Notice of leaseholder's claim* must contain information about the house sufficiently precise to identify all the property to which the claim extends; the rateable value of the house and premises on various dates; particulars of the tenancy; the date on which the tenant acquired the tendancy; the periods in the last 10 years during which the tenant has and has not occupied the house as his residence.

If, for any reason, a tenant cannot trace his landlord, he may apply to the High Court and they will advise him what to do. He will not lose his rights.

effect of tenant's notice
Unless the landlord successfully opposes the tenant's application, he is bound to convey the freehold to the tenant or grant him an extended lease. The notice, in effect, operates like a contract between the landlord and the tenant.

If a landlord has contracted to sell the freehold to a third party prior to his tenant claiming to buy the freehold, the tenant's rights are unaffected. The contract between the landlord and the third party disappears and the landlord must convey to the tenant; similarly if the tenant has claimed an extended lease, the new landlord must grant it.

withdrawing
Where the tenant is buying the freehold, once a price has been fixed or agreed, the tenant has a period of one month in which he may withdraw his notice. To withdraw, the must give notice in writing to his landlord (and all superior landlords if he is a sub-tenant). Such notice has the effect of cancelling the tenant's previous claim to buy the freehold. He must however pay any costs incurred by his landlord (or superior landlords). He loses the right to claim the freehold for the next three years, but the right to claim an extension of his lease is not lost.

the landlord's reply

Within 2 months of being served with a tenant's notice, a landlord (or, if the notice is served by a sub-tenant, the reversioner) must serve his notice in reply to the tenant. The form a landlord must use is form 2 (*Notice in reply to leaseholder's claim*). This form contains five paragraphs together with five explanatory notes (referred to in the margin of the form):

Paragraph 1:   simply states that the landlord (or reversioner) has received a copy of the tenant's notice claiming to buy the freehold or extend his lease.

Paragraph 2:   states whether the tenant's claim is admitted or not and if not, the grounds on which the landlord opposes the claim. A landlord who admits a tenant's claim cannot later dispute it unless he shows that the tenant has misled him in some way.

Paragraph 3:   specifies whether any claim will be made to recover possession for the purposes of redevelopment or for the purpose of housing the landlord or an adult member of his family.

Paragraph 4:   in certain circumstances a landlord can require the tenant to take additional premises or to exclude certain premises from his claim. A landlord here gives the tenant notice of this.

Paragraph 5:   applies only to notices served by a reversioner where the tenant making the claim is a sub-tenant.

conveyancing procedure

The steps necessary to complete the conveyance or transfer of the freehold or the grant of an extended lease to a tenant are laid down in the Leasehold Reform (Enfranchisement and Extension) Regulations 1967. The procedure laid down by the Regulations may be varied by agreement.

Where a claim is made by a sub-tenant, the word landlord refers to the reversioner who conducts the sale or grant on behalf of superior landlords.

buying the freehold

(i) *Deposit:*   At any time after receiving a tenant's notice a landlord may, in writing, ask the tenant to pay a deposit of either not more than £25 or three times the tenant's annual rent, whichever is the greater.

The tenant has 14 days in which to comply.

(ii) *Evidence of right to enfranchise:*   The landlord may ask the tenant to prove his title to the tenancy and require the tenant to produce a statutory declaration giving details of his three years' occupation of the property. The tenant should ask a solicitor how to go about obtaining such a statutory declaration – he will have to swear it before a solicitor, anyway.

The tenant has 21 days to comply with the request.

(iii) *Proof of the landlord's title:* A tenant may, by notice in writing, require the landlord to deduce title to the freehold. This means that the landlord has to show who owns the freehold and whether or not it is subject to incumbrances. In the case of registered land, title is deduced by the landlord giving the tenant an authority to inspect the register, office copies of the entries on the register, and evidence of rights about which the register is not conclusive. (The procedure for buying and selling registered land is explained in the Consumer Publication *The legal side of buying a house.*) If title to the property is not registered, the landlord must provide the tenant with an abstract or epitome of his title. He should obtain the advice of a solicitor as to what the abstract or epitome should contain.

(iv) *Requisitions on title:* These are questions asked in writing by or on behalf of a buyer of property about the seller's ownership of it. This is generally done by using a standard form ('Conveyancing 28B') containing a number of questions, the irrelevant ones of which the buyer crosses out; the landlord has to reply to the ones left in the form.

The tenant has to make his requisitions within 14 days of the date the landlord deduced title. The landlord must reply to the tenant's requisitions within 14 days of receiving them.

(v) *Contents and preparation of the transfer (registered land) or conveyance (unregistered land):* The Regulations specify time limits within which each party must let the other know of any provisions (such as to rights of way or restriction on the use of the property) to be included in the transfer or conveyance. The tenant may give the landlord notice asking him to specify any such provisions such as, for example, to give details of any rights of way.

The landlord has 4 weeks in which to supply the relevant information. A landlord may similarly ask the tenant for details and the tenant has 4 weeks to reply.

The tenant has the task of preparing the transfer or conveyance. He must deliver a draft transfer or conveyance to the landlord (or his solicitor) at least 14 days before the date fixed for completion. The draft transfer or conveyance, when agreed, must be engrossed by the tenant and delivered to the landlord, a reasonable time before completion.

A tenant may be required to execute as many copies of the transfer or conveyance as the landlord reasonably requires.

(vi) *Completion:* After one month from the date on which the price the tenant has to pay has been determined, either the tenant or the landlord may give the other notice in writing requiring him to complete the transaction. The completion date is then set at the first working day after 4 weeks from the day the notice expires.

If completion is delayed for any reason, the tenant must go on paying rent unless the landlord opts to take interest at 2% above the current bank base rate on the unpaid purchase money. Rent or interest remains payable until the day of actual completion.

Where completion is delayed solely because of the landlord's fault, the tenant may, instead:
○ at his own risk, deposit the price or the balance of the price, at any bank in England or Wales; and
○ give notice in writing of such deposit to the landlord or his solicitor.

The landlord has to accept such interest as is actually earned (which may be less than the 'plus 2%' he would be entitled to).

(vii) *Apportionment of rent and outgoings:* The tenant has to pay rent up to the date of actual completion and after that all outgoings, for instance rates. Any current rent and rates outstanding at the date of completion are to be apportioned on a daily basis.

(viii) *Time limits:* A reversioner may serve notice on the tenant specifying that the above time limits be doubled in so far as he is concerned: the time limits remain the same for the tenant.

(ix) *Failure to comply with obligations:* If either party fails to comply with his obligations, the other may serve a notice on the defaulting party giving him 2 months to make good his default.

If the tenant does not obey the notice, any deposit he has paid is forfeit, that is, the landlord can keep it and is released from his obligations, and the tenant must pay the landlord's reasonable costs.

If the landlord is in default and does not comply with the notice, the tenant may recover his deposit and the landlord loses his right to recover his costs from the tenant. The tenant may then have to apply to the court if the landlord continues to be unhelpful.

claiming the grant of an extended lease

The procedure is much the same as for buying the freehold with obvious modifications to take account of the fact that only a 50-year lease is being granted.

There are, however, the following material differences:

(i) *Terms of the new tenancy:*   Either party is required to state, by notice, what modifications (other than rent) are to be made to the terms of the existing tenancy. The landlord has the right to include restrictions on the use of the property in certain circumstances, for example, where it is necessary for the benefit of the neighbourhood generally, a special management scheme may be set up.

(ii) *Preparation of the lease:*   Within 8 weeks of either party giving notice, the landlord must send a draft lease to the tenant who has 21 days to approve it with or without amendments. The landlord has to produce an engrossment of the lease and the required counterpart copies of it.

(iii) *Completion:*   When the time limit for the approval of the draft lease has elapsed, either party may serve notice in writing on the other, requiring completion of the lease. The completion date is then set as the first working day after the expiration of 4 weeks from the date notice is given.

costs

A tenant who exercises his rights under the Act has to meet the following items of expenditure:

○ The landlord's reasonable costs of investigating his right to the freehold or an extended lease.

○ The landlord's reasonable costs incurred in having a valuation of the house made; the cost of preparing the conveyance or transfer or lease.
○ The landlord's reasonable costs of deducing title to the freehold, where appropriate.
○ Stamp duty on the transfer or conveyance or lease, where appropriate (at present, where the purchase price is over £30,000).
○ Land Registry fees (for registered land only), to register his interest if he becomes the freeholder or takes a lease of more than 21 years.

A landlord is entitled to refuse to execute a new, extended lease for a tenant unless:

(a) all rent due is paid; *and*
(b) all costs recoverable by the landlord are paid; *and*
(c) any other sums that are due to the landlord (for example service charges) are paid.

Where a sub-tenant exercises his rights under the Act, he is liable to pay the reasonable costs of all superior landlords, not just those of the reversioner. (He deals with only one person, who conducts the landlord's side of things, but other 'landlords' are involved, as they too are being bought out.)

Housing booklet No 9 *Leasehold Reform* published by the Department of the Environment and Welsh Office contains fifty questions and answers as a guide for leaseholders and landlords.

renting and letting in the public sector

Tenants in the public and quasi-public sector who are 'secure tenants' are given a number of rights by the Housing Act 1980, the Housing and Building Control Act 1984 and the Housing Defects Act 1984. These rights include security of tenure, the right to take lodgers and to sub-let (with the landlord's consent), the right to carry out repairs, and the right to be furnished with information about the landlord's obligations under the tenancy. Most, though not all, secure tenants also have the right to buy their homes and to obtain financial assistance in doing so.

Basically, a secure tenant is someone who rents a dwelling-house from a designated landlord and who occupies it as his only or principal home. It is irrelevant whether he holds under a lease or a licence: the Housing Act gives the same protection to licensees as to tenants, except where a licence is given as a temporary expedient to someone who enters land as a trespasser.

dwelling-house
For these purposes, a dwelling-house is defined as a house or part of a house. The tenancy or licence must be of accommodation let as a separate dwelling.

'designated' landlord
The landlord must be one of the following bodies:

○ a local authority, which includes a county, district or London borough council, the Common Council of the City of London, the Council of the Isles of Scilly

○ the Commission for the New Towns
○ an urban development corporation (established under the Local Government, Planning and Land Act 1980)
○ a development corporation (a statutory body set up to stimulate growth in new towns)
○ the Housing Corporation (Maple House, 149 Tottenham Court Road, London W1P 0BN, telephone 01-387 9466)
○ a housing trust which is a charity (the Charity Commissioners, telephone 01-214 6000, keep a register of all charities)
○ the Development Board for Rural Wales
○ a housing management co-operative (approved by the Secretary of State as suitable to exercise the powers of the local housing authority)
○ a housing association registered under the Housing Associations Act 1985 other than a co-operative housing association
○ an unregistered housing association which is a co-operative housing association. (Tenants of co-operative housing associations enjoy fewer rights than secure tenants of other landlords.)

the tenant
The tenant must be an individual and must occupy the dwelling-house as his only or principal home. If there is a joint tenancy, each tenant must be an individual and at least one must live in the property. A limited company cannot be a secure tenant.

exceptions

The following tenancies or licences are not secure tenancies:

○ *long leases:* granted for 21 years or more, whether or not they can be terminated before the end of the term by the tenant serving a notice or by the landlord bringing forfeiture proceedings.
○ *premises occupied in connection with employment:* where the tenant is required by his contract of employment to occupy the dwelling-house for the better performance of his duties.

The Act deals specifically with members of the police force and firemen. The former are not secure tenants if the accommodation is provided free of rent and rates; the latter are excluded where their contract of employment requires them to live in close proximity to a particular fire station and a dwelling-house was let to them in consequence of that requirement.

○ *land acquired for development:* if the landlord acquires land for development but then lets it as temporary housing accommodation pending the development in question, there will be no secure tenancy.

○ *accommodation for homeless persons:* a person will not qualify as a secure tenant who is accommodated temporarily while the local authority considers whether there is a duty to house him under the 'housing the homeless' provisions in Part III of the Housing Act 1985. The accommodation may cease to be temporary for these purposes if the tenant stays there for more than a year.

○ *temporary accommodation for people taking up employment:* a person will not qualify as a secure tenant who is given accommodation by a local authority in order to enable him to take up a new job. He may become a secure tenant if he remains in the property for more than a year.

○ *short-term arrangements:* private sector bodies may let property to a landlord in the public sector to be used as temporary housing accommodation. Tenancies granted in such circumstances by the public sector landlord are not secure tenancies.

○ *temporary accommodation during works:* if a person is provided with temporary accommodation while his actual home is being repaired, and he is not a secure tenant of that home, there will not be a secure tenancy.

○ *agricultural holdings, licensed premises and almshouses*

○ *student lettings:* a letting by one of the designated landlords to a student who attends a full-time course at a university, polytechnic or other college is not normally a secure tenancy, but the landlord must give notice to the student explaining the exemption.

If a student's course finishes or he leaves it, the occupancy will become a secure tenancy after six months from the date the student's course finished or he left it. It is therefore important for the landlord to get possession as soon as he knows that either of these circumstances has arisen.

○ *tenancies under the Landlord and Tenant Act 1954:* tenancies of premises occupied for business purposes are not secure tenancies.

○ *succession:* after there has been one succession to a secure tenancy, the status of secure tenancy comes to an end.
○ *assignment:* in general, assignments of secure tenancies are not permitted and a tenancy will cease to be a secure tenancy if it is assigned. There are three exceptions to this. A tenancy may sometimes be assigned by way of exchange; it may be assigned under a court order during divorce proceedings; and it may be handed over (assigned) to a person who would be entitled to succeed to the secure tenancy on the death of the secure tenant.

the rights of a secure tenant (including a licensee)

None of the tenant's rights can be excluded by the tenancy agreement.

the right to exchange
All secure tenants may exchange their homes with other secure tenants. There is no need for the two secure tenants to have the same landlord. Obtaining the landlord's consent is a pre-condition to exchange; where the secure tenants have different landlords, the consent of both landlords is required.

The landlord may refuse consent only on one of the grounds listed below, and must give his tenant notice of such refusal within 42 days of the tenant applying for consent. If the consent is withheld for some other reason, it will be treated as having been given. When giving consent, the landlord may impose a condition on the tenant that any arrears of rent must be paid or that any breaches of the terms of the tenancy must be remedied. No other conditions may be imposed.

Consent to exchange can be refused if:

○ a possession order has been made, or possession proceedings have been started, against the landlord's existing tenant or the person with whom he wants to exchange ('the tenant by way of exchange') on one of the grounds relating to a tenant's default under his lease (failure to pay rent, damage to furniture and so on)

○ the tenant by way of exchange would have substantially more accommodation than he reasonably requires or the accommodation is too small for his and his family's needs

○ the dwelling-house is let by a charity and occupation by the proposed tenant by way of exchange would result in a breach of the charity's objects

○ the landlord is a housing association or housing trust which lets the property only to people whose circumstances (other than financial circumstances) make them difficult to house and the exchange would mean that such a person would no longer live in the property

○ the property is specially adapted for a physically disabled person and the result of the exchange would be that such a person would no longer occupy the property

○ the property is one of a group set up for people with special needs near to specially provided facilities or social services and the exchange would mean the property would no longer be occupied by a person with such special needs

○ the property is within the curtilage of a building held by a landlord for non-residential purposes and is let to an employee of either the landlord or a local authority, new town or urban development corporation, governors of an aided school or the Development Board for Rural Wales, and the employee holds his secure tenancy in consequence of his employment (if the employee occupies the property for the better fulfilment of his job, he does not have a secure tenancy, only a service occupancy).

A secure tenant should not take any lump sum payment on exchange. If he does, the landlord may be able to recover possession and would not have to provide alternative accommodation.

the right to take in lodgers
A secure tenant may take in lodgers, without obtaining the landlord's prior consent. However, if the dwelling becomes overcrowded within the meaning of the Housing Act 1985 as a consequence, the landlord may be entitled to obtain possession of it.

the right to sub-let

Every secure tenant has the right to sub-let part of his home. He must first obtain his landlord's consent, which cannot be unreasonably withheld. If it is withheld, the consent is treated as having been given. The onus is on the landlord to show that the withholding was not unreasonable.

If the landlord refuses consent, the tenant can demand a written statement of the reasons for such refusal. If the landlord gives consent conditionally (for example, subject to the tenant doing certain repairs) the consent takes effect as though the condition did not exist. If the landlord neither gives nor refuses consent but merely remains silent, he will be deemed to have withheld consent unreasonably.

Where a secure tenant feels that his landlord has unreasonably refused consent or has remained silent, the most sensible thing for him to do is to apply to the county court for a declaration of consent having been unreasonably withheld. He may then sub-let without risk of being in breach of the terms of his lease.

If a secure tenant sub-lets the whole of his home, he is no longer a secure tenant because he will not be in occupation of any part of the premises, and will lose the protection of the Housing Act. The sub-tenant in such circumstances would not qualify as a secure tenant either.

the right to carry out repairs

The landlord's repairing obligations may be specifically mentioned in the tenancy agreement but, in any event, if the tenancy is for seven years or less, the Landlord and Tenant Act 1985 makes the landlord (that is, the council, if a council tenancy) liable

○ to keep in repair the structure and exterior of the dwelling-house (including drains, gutters and pipes)
○ to keep in repair and proper working order the installations in the dwelling-house for the supply of water, gas and electricity and for sanitation (including basins, sinks, baths and sanitary conveniences, but not other fixtures, fittings and appliances for making use of the supply of water, gas or electricity; that means that the landlord is not liable, for example, for the electric or gas fire itself, but is for the electricity supply and gas pipes)

○ to keep in repair and proper working order the installations in the dwelling-house for space heating and heating water.

The landlord cannot contract out of these responsibilities, and a clause in the tenancy agreement requiring the tenant to perform these tasks is of no effect.

The Secretary of State is given power to draw up a scheme whereby the tenant is entitled to carry out repairs which are the responsibility of the landlord, and to recover the cost of doing so from the landlord. One such scheme has so far been drawn up.

The first 'right to repair' scheme came into effect at the beginning of 1986. This scheme is limited to 'qualifying repairs' which means any repairs for which the landlord is responsible other than repairs to the structure and exterior of a flat.

Under the scheme, the tenant must begin by serving a notice on the landlord describing the proposed works, why they are needed and the materials to be used. The landlord must then reply within 21 days either granting or refusing the tenant's repair claim. The landlord may refuse the claim in the following circumstances:

○ where the landlord's costs would be more than £200
○ where the landlord intends to carry out the work within 28 days of the claim
○ where the works are not reasonably necessary for the personal comfort or safety of the tenant and those living with him and the landlord intends to carry them out within one year as part of a planned programme of repair
○ where the works would infringe the terms of any guarantee of which the landlord has the benefit
○ where the tenant has unreasonably failed to provide the landlord with access to inspect the site for the works.

The landlord must refuse the claim in the following circumstances:

○ where the landlord's costs would be less than £20
○ where the works do not constitute a qualifying repair
○ where the works if carried out using the materials specified would not, in the landlord's opinion, satisfactorily remedy the lack of repair.

If the landlord accepts the claim, he (or it: the local authority or similar body) must serve a notice on the tenant specifying:

○ the date by which a claim for compensation must be made following completion of the work

○ the amount that it would cost the authority to carry out the works itself

○ the percentage of those costs that the authority is prepared to pay (this figure must not be less than 75% and may be up to 100%)

○ any modifications of the work and/or materials which it requires.

The tenant may then proceed to carry out the work in question and to make a claim to the landlord for payment. The landlord must then pay the tenant except in a few specified circumstances (for example, if the work has not been done satisfactorily).

If the landlord refuses to reply to the tenant's notice, the tenant may serve a 'default notice' on the landlord. If he still receives no reply within seven days, he may proceed with the works and claim the cost, if necessary through the court, up to a maximum of £200, from the landlord.

Any disputes that arise may be referred by either party to the county court.

Quite apart from the right of the tenant to carry out certain repairs himself and to recover the cost from the landlord, the tenant may also bring an action directly against the landlord for failure to comply with its repairing obligations. In particular, he may seek an order from the county court (under the Landlord and Tenant Act 1985) requiring the landlord to carry out the repairs in question. This may be the best tactic if the tenant cannot afford to do the work himself.

the right to make improvements

This right is subject to the tenant first obtaining the landlord's consent. If consent is withheld, the landlord must give the tenant a written statement explaining why. Consent must not be unreasonably withheld, and if it is it will be deemed to have been given. The onus is on the landlord to show that the withholding of consent is reasonable.

If the landlord gives consent to the improvements, it may impose conditions providing that they are reasonable. The Housing Act

1985 enables the landlord to repay some or all of the costs of the improvement to the secure tenant at or after the end of the tenancy ('enables' because this gives the local authority statutory power to make such payments which otherwise they would lack). There is, however, no duty to do so. The landlord may do so where it gave consent to the improvement and the improvement materially added to the price the property would be expected to fetch if sold or rented on the open market.

A landlord is not allowed to increase the rent to take account of a tenant's improvements except to the extent that the tenant did not bear the cost of them himself. However, where the tenant pays rent inclusive of rates, he will have to bear the expense of any increase in rates resulting from the improvements. A secure tenant's successor is also protected from any increase in rent because of improvements made by his predecessor. Only when the successor's tenancy ends can the landlord increase the rent payable in respect of the improved property.

the right to information

Landlords of dwelling-houses let under secure tenancies must publish information from time to time explaining in simple terms

○ the express terms of its secure tenancies
○ the 'right to buy' provisions contained in the Housing Act 1985
○ the landlord's repairing obligations under the Landlord and Tenant Act 1985.

The landlord must supply its secure tenants with a copy of this information and a written statement of the terms of the tenancy in so far as they do not appear in the lease or written tenancy agreement and are not implied by law. This statement must be supplied when the tenancy is granted or as soon as practicable thereafter.

Public sector landlords must also publish a summary of their rules for determining priority between applicants for housing, and for dealing with applications by secure tenants to move to other dwelling-houses let under secure tenancies. These rules must be made available for inspection at the landlord's principal office at all reasonable hours, free of charge.

Provision also exists for the Secretary of State to require landlords to give information to tenants regarding charges made in respect of heating and the supply of hot water, where this is provided in accordance with a local communal heating scheme. As yet, the Secretary of State has not brought this provision into effect.

the right to be consulted

The secure tenant has the right to be consulted by his landlord on most aspects of housing management. If a landlord proposes to make substantial alterations to the layout of an estate, for instance, the tenants must be consulted, and their views considered before a decision is taken. Landlords must, on request, provide their secure tenants with details of their consultation procedure.

Similarly, a landlord may not vary the terms of a secure tenancy, except

○ by agreement with the tenant;

○ in accordance with the terms of the tenancy in relation to payments for rent, rates and services; or

○ by notice of variation in the case of a periodic tenancy. In this case, the landlord serves a preliminary notice of the variation on the tenant, explaining the substance of the variation and asking the tenant for his comments. After considering the tenant's comments, the landlord serves a further notice of variation which states the date on which the variation is to take effect: this must be either when a rental period expires or after four weeks, whichever is longer. The tenant's sole remedy, if he objects to the variation, is to give notice to quit. The landlord does not need to observe the procedure of a preliminary notice when issuing a variation notice regarding payments in respect of rent, rates or services.

exception

The rights just described – that is, the rights to assign, sublet, repair, improve, information and consultation – do not apply to tenants of co-operative housing associations.

security of tenure

Secure tenants enjoy security of tenure analogous to that of private sector regulated tenants under the Rent Act 1977. The tenant may go on living in his home after his contractual right to be there has ended and the landlord needs a court order to regain possession which will be granted only in certain prescribed circumstances.

the right to remain in possession

When a secure tenant's original periodic tenancy or fixed-term tenancy or licence agreement comes to an end, he becomes entitled to a statutory periodic tenancy: he continues on the same terms as the original secure tenancy in so far as these terms are compatible with a periodic tenancy. The notional length of the periodic tenancy will depend on how the tenant has been paying rent: if monthly, the periodic tenancy will be a monthly one; if weekly there will be a weekly periodic tenancy and so on.

If the secure tenant was originally a periodic tenant there will be little change in his position, except that the landlord's right to end the new statutory periodic tenancy by notice to quit is restricted: the landlord can only end the tenancy in the prescribed circumstances stated in the above paragraph.

successors

If a secure tenant dies (before or after the end of the original occupation agreement), generally the tenancy is automatically transferred to the person entitled to succeed to the secure tenancy under the 1985 Act. But unlike statutory tenancies under the Rent Act, there is only one automatic successor; nothing in the Act, however, prevents a landlord from agreeing to a second succession.

A person may succeed a secure tenant if at the time of the secure tenant's death he/she occupied the dwelling-house as his or her only or principal home and is either

○ the secure tenant's husband or wife; or
○ another member of the secure tenant's family and has lived with the secure tenant throughout the 12 months up to the secure tenant's death.

The other members of the secure tenant's family are: the so-called 'common-law' husband or wife, parents, grandparents, grand-children, children, brothers and sisters, uncles and aunts, nephews and nieces; relations by marriage, illegitimate children and adopted children are also included.

A secure tenant's spouse takes precedence over other members of the family. If two or more members of the family are entitled to succeed to the secure tenancy and cannot agree between themselves who is to take it, the landlord can decide who is to be the successor.

no successors

In the following circumstances there will be no automatic transfer on the death of the secure tenant:

○ where there has already been an automatic transfer to a secure tenant's spouse or a member of his family; or

○ where the deceased secure tenant acquired the tenancy under the will or on the intestacy of the previous tenant; or

○ on the death of a surviving joint tenant (where there is a joint tenancy and one tenant dies, the tenancy automatically passes to the survivor under the general law); or

○ where there was originally a fixed term or periodic tenancy which has been assigned (sold or exchanged). Although the assignee will be statutorily entitled to a periodic tenancy when the original term ends, there is no automatic transfer on his death.

Assignees who take over the secure tenancy under a property transfer order on or after divorce, nullity or judicial separation, do not count as assignees for this purpose. However, if the other party to the marriage had acquired the tenancy by assignment there will be no rights of succession.

how to end a secure tenancy

Basically, a secure tenancy can be ended by:

○ a periodic tenant serving a notice to quit on the landlord;
○ agreement between the landlord and tenant;
○ the secure tenant exercising his 'right to buy';
○ the landlord obtaining a court order enforcing a right to forfeit his tenant's lease and re-enter the property. (However, a periodic tenancy would automatically arise and the tenant would not have to move out unless the landlord obtains a court order for possession);
○ a landlord obtaining an order for possession from the court. Before the court will grant such an order, a landlord must establish one of the grounds for possession listed in the Housing Act 1985.

A landlord who wishes to obtain a court order for possession must first serve on the tenant notice in the prescribed form. There are two forms: one for use where the secure tenant has a periodic tenancy, the other for use where the landlord wants to end a fixed term tenancy under a proviso for re-entry and forfeiture and regain possession.

Both state the name(s) of the secure tenant(s), the name of the landlord and address of the property, the ground on which possession is sought and the landlord's reasons for taking action to recover possession. There are extensive notes to explain the importance of the notice to the recipient. A notice in respect of a periodic tenancy also gives a date before which court proceedings cannot be brought.

the statutory grounds for obtaining possession

The Housing Act 1985 lays down the grounds on which a landlord may recover possession.

reasonableness
The court will grant an order for possession on any one of the following grounds if it is reasonable to do so. (The court must consider reasonableness separately from the grounds.)

GROUND 1: Any rent lawfully due from a tenant has not been paid, or any obligation (such as to repair) has been broken or not performed. A tenant may avoid a possession order if he makes good his breach of covenant or pays off all arrears of rent before court proceedings start. Mostly councils do not want to obtain possession but to get the arrears paid. Orders are, therefore, often suspended, pending the payment of the arrears at so-much per week in addition to current rent. (But even if the full amount of the arrears is paid off, the tenant may still be liable for the costs of the local authority in bringing the action unless they agree not to proceed with it.)

GROUND 2: The tenant or any person living with him has been guilty of conduct which constitutes a nuisance or annoyance to neighbours or has been convicted of using the dwelling-house (or allowing it to be used) for immoral or illegal purposes.

GROUND 3: The condition of the dwelling-house or any of the common parts has deteriorated due to the act or default (for example, not carrying out repairs) of the tenant or any person living with him. If the tenant has a lodger or sub-tenant who has caused the deterioration, the landlord has to show that the tenant has not taken reasonable steps to remove the lodger or sub-tenant.

GROUND 4: The tenant or someone living with him has damaged furniture provided by the landlord. Again, if the furniture has been damaged by a lodger or sub-tenant, the landlord has to show that the tenant has not taken reasonable steps to remove him.

GROUND 5: The tenant induced the landlord to grant him the tenancy by making false statements.

GROUND 6: The tenant has acquired his home by way of exchange and a premium was paid either to or by him, by or to the other party.

GROUND 7: The landlord is one of the following bodies

− a local authority
− a new town or urban development corporation
− the Commission for the New Towns
− the governors of an aided school
− the Development Board for Rural Wales

and the tenant's dwelling-house is part of property used mainly for non-residential purposes and the tenant's conduct or that of a person living with him makes it wrong for him to continue to occupy. In this case, the tenancy must have been originally granted as a result of his employment with the landlord.

GROUND 8: The tenant occupies (or the previous tenant occupied) the dwelling-house while works are (or were) executed on his previous home and

○ he (or the previous tenant) was a secure tenant of the previous home; and
○ he (or the previous tenant) promised to leave the present premises when the works on his previous home were finished; and
○ the works are now finished.

alternative accommodation
A landlord may obtain a court order for possession on one of the following grounds, if suitable alternative accommodation will be available to the tenant when the order is to take effect.

Alternative accommodation is suitable if it is let on a secure or protected tenancy and, in the opinion of the court, reasonably suitable to the needs of the tenant and his family. In determining this the court must have regard to

○ the nature of the accommodation which the landlord in practice allocates to someone with similar needs;
○ the distance of the accommodation from the workplace or school/college, and so on, of the tenant and any members of his family;
○ the distance of the accommodation from the home of any member of the tenant's family where being near is essential to the well-being of either the tenant or the member of his family;
○ the extent of the accommodation and the means of the tenant and his family;
○ the terms on which the accommodation is available and the terms of the secure tenancy;
○ where furniture is provided under the secure tenancy, whether it is to be provided for the tenant in the alternative accommodation and, if so, the nature of that furniture.

Where the landlord is not a local authority and produces a certificate from the local authority saying that they will provide suitable accommodation, this is conclusive that such accommodation will be available. Local authorities are normally reluctant to give such certificates.

The grounds for possession are:

GROUND 9:   The dwelling-house is overcrowded within the meaning of Part x of the Housing Act 1985.

GROUND 10:   The landlord intends, within a reasonable time of obtaining possession, to demolish or reconstruct the building or carry out work on the building (or on land let with it) and cannot reasonably do so without obtaining possession of the secure tenant's home. There must be a firm intention to redevelop on the part of the landlord, not merely some vague plan for the future. The court might, for example, ask the landlord to produce builders' estimates.

GROUND 10A: The dwelling-house is in an area which is the subject of a redevelopment scheme within the terms of the Housing and Planning Act 1986.

GROUND 11:   The landlord is a charity and the tenant's continued occupation of the property conflicts with the objects of the charity.

reasonableness and alternative accommodation
To obtain possession on one of the following grounds, the landlord must satisfy the court also that it is reasonable to make an order for possession, not only that suitable alternative accommodation will be available to the tenant when the order becomes effective.

GROUND 12:   The tenant was formerly an employee of the present landlord (or of one of the bodies specified in GROUND 7) and the dwelling-house is within the curtilage of a building consisting mainly of accommodation held by the landlord for non-housing purposes and is reasonably needed for one of its employees (or an employee of one of the specified bodies) in the future.

GROUND 13:   The tenant occupies property specifically adapted for use by a physically disabled person, there is no longer a disabled person living there, and the landlord wants possession for occupation by such a person.

GROUND 14:   The landlord is a housing association which lets only to people whose circumstances (other than financial) make it especially difficult for them to satisfy their need for housing, there is now no longer anyone with special circumstances living in the property or the present tenant has received a firm offer of suitable alternative accommodation from a local authority, and the premises are required to house someone with special circumstances.

GROUND 15:   The dwelling-house is one of a group which the landlord lets to people with special needs, *and*
a social service or special facility is provided in close proximity to assist the tenants, *and*
the dwelling-house is not occupied by a person with special needs, *and*
the landlord requires the property for a person with special needs to live in.

So, a landlord who lets houses in a complex specially designed for the elderly may regain possession on this ground.

GROUND 16:   The tenant has succeeded to the secure tenancy and the property is more extensive than is reasonably required by him. The court must take account of the tenant's age, the length of occupation of the dwelling, and any financial or other support given by the tenant to the previous tenant. To recover possession on this ground, the landlord must bring proceedings between six and twelve months from the death of the previous tenant. A spouse of the deceased tenant cannot be dispossessed on this ground.

the right to buy

Most secure tenants (that includes the average council tenant) have the right to buy their homes. This right is contained in the Housing Act 1985. The Act excludes the following secure tenancies from the right to buy provisions:

○ lettings by a housing trust or housing association where the landlord is a charity
○ lettings by co-operative housing associations or other housing associations which have at no point received public funds
○ lettings by landlords with an insufficient interest (that is, a landlord who does not own the freehold or a sufficiently long leasehold to grant a long lease to the tenant)
○ lettings of properties which are held mainly for non-housing purposes and which were let to the tenant or his predecessor in connection with his employment
○ certain lettings of properties specially adapted for physically disabled people, or adapted for use by the elderly
○ lettings of sheltered accommodation for the mentally disordered
○ certain lettings by the Crown.

The Housing Act also provides that the right to buy cannot be exercised by a tenant against whom an order for possession has been made, or an undischarged bankrupt, or anyone involved in bankruptcy proceedings, or a tenant who has made a composition or arrangement with his creditors the terms of which remain to be fulfilled.

the time condition
The tenant must have been a tenant of a public sector landlord for at least 2 years. The two-year period does not need to be spent in the same dwelling or as a tenant of the same landlord. The important point is that the two years or more should have been spent as a public sector tenant.

joint tenants and members of the family
When two or more secure joint tenants are entitled to buy their home, the right belongs to them all jointly. At least one of these

joint tenants must occupy the dwelling as his only or principal home. Only one of the joint tenants needs to have satisfied the time condition.

A secure tenant may, when he gives notice of his intention to buy, require that up to 3 members of his family (who need not be joint tenants) be allowed to buy with him. The secure tenant can join his spouse or any member of the family who lives and has for the past 12 months lived with him, or – if the family member has not lived with the tenant – if the landlord gives his consent to the family member joining in the purchase.

what a secure tenant can buy

If the tenant's home is a flat, he can only buy a long lease, never the freehold; if it is a house, he can buy the freehold or long lease.

houses

If the secure tenant lives in a house and the landlord owns the freehold, the tenant is entitled to acquire the freehold interest. If the landlord only owns a leasehold interest, the tenant will be granted a long lease of the house at a nominal rent; normally the lease will be for a period of at least 125 years, although sometimes it will be for less (for instance, where the landlord's own interest is for a shorter period). A tenant who is granted a long lease might at a later date be able to enfranchise his interest and acquire the freehold under the Leasehold Reform Act 1967, even where the freehold is owned by someone in the private sector.

flats

If the secure tenant lives in a flat, he will be granted a long lease at a nominal rent; again the lease will normally be for at least 125 years, although sometimes it may be for less (where the landlord had less).

The following provisions will be contained (or implied) in the lease:

○ rights to the enjoyment of common parts previously enjoyed by the secure tenant
○ that the landlord will keep the structure and exterior of the

dwelling-house in repair and make good any defect affecting that structure, unless details of such defects have been given to the tenant

○ indemnity by the tenant in respect of breach of restrictive covenants affecting the landlord
○ covenant by the tenant to keep the interior in good repair
○ rights of support, passage of water, gas, electricity, etc
○ necessary rights of way
○ other rights enjoyed by the tenant when he gave notice of intent to buy, insofar as the landlord can grant them.

Some of these rights (such as the last three) will also be included in a conveyance of the freehold of a house to a secure tenant who is exercising his right to buy, where appropriate.

calculating the price
The Housing Act 1985 lays down the method for calculating the price a secure tenant must pay when buying his home. The formula is:

**value of dwelling-house at relevant time
minus discount entitlement**

the value of the dwelling-house
The value of the dwelling-house must be assessed at the 'relevant time', that is the date at which the secure tenant serves a notice on the landlord of his intention to buy.

The value of the dwelling-house means the price which it would realise if sold on the open market by a willing seller, at the relevant time. In the case of a sale of the freehold interest, the following assumptions are made:

○ the vendor is selling the freehold with vacant possession;
○ neither the tenant nor a member of his family living there with him wants to buy;
○ the property is to be conveyed subject only to rights and burdens which may be imposed under the Housing Act 1985. These include necessary rights of way, rights of support and light and passage of water, gas and electricity, sewage and so on.

On the grant of a long lease (flat, or a house where the landlord owns only a leasehold interest) the assumptions are that:

○ the ground rent will not exceed £10 per annum;
○ where the landlord has an interest of more than 125 years plus 5 days, he is granting a lease of 125 years with vacant possession;
○ where the landlord has an interest of less than 125 years and 5 days, he is granting a lease equal to the remainder of his own term less 5 days, with vacant possession;
○ neither the tenant nor a member of his family living there with him wants to take the lease;
○ the grant is on the terms specified in the Housing Act 1985.

The effect of these assumptions is to lower the price which the property would otherwise realise if sold to the secure tenant.

In making the valuation, any improvements made by the secure tenant or a member of his family or predecessors (if they would have been secure tenants) are ignored.

In the first instance, it is the responsibility of the landlord to determine the value of the dwelling-house at the relevant time. A landlord may ask the district valuer to help him in this respect. If the district valuer is not initially consulted, or the tenant disagrees with the value attributed to the dwelling by the landlord or the district valuer, the tenant has the right to require a revaluation to be carried out by another officer from the district valuer's office. A tenant must serve written notice on his landlord within 3 months of receiving his landlord's valuation, requiring the district valuer's involvement. (Standard forms for this are available from law stationers.)

discount entitlement
The discount entitlement is calculated according to the length of time the secure tenant has been a public sector tenant. Periods as a tenant of several public sector landlords – not just the one from which the tenant wishes to buy – may be taken into account. Time spent by members of the secure tenant's family may also be taken into account, although it is not possible to add together different people's discount entitlements. If there is a secure joint tenancy, the discount is based on whichever of the joint tenants is entitled to the largest amount.

The discount entitlement is as follows:

○ if the tenant has been a public sector tenant for two years, 32% of the value of the dwelling-house at the relevant time
○ for every full year thereafter, an extra 1% is added to the amount of the discount, subject to a maximum of 60%
○ the maximum discount allowable is £25,000
○ a discount has to stop short of resulting in the tenant paying less for his home than it cost the landlord to build it, where the building work took place after 1 April 1974.

As an example of discount entitlement, let us assume that Mr Samuel Taylor has lived in his council house for 10 years and at the date he makes his application it is valued at £20,000. He will pay £20,000 less £8,000 (discount of 40%) amounting to £12,000.
(*Note*: Under the Housing and Planning Act 1986, the Secretary of State has been given power to allow larger discounts for flats than for houses. The Act provides that an initial discount of 44%, plus 2% for every full year thereafter, up to a maximum of 70%, may be given. So far, this power has not been exercised.)

losing the discount
A secure tenant's discount will be reduced if he has bought previously and received a discount on that occasion (or if he has received a discount when acquiring a shared ownership lease; shared ownership is explained later on in this book). Similarly, the discount will be reduced where the tenant's spouse or other joint purchaser has received discount on a prior occasion.

A secure tenant who buys his home at discount and then sells it to a third party within the next five years is liable to repay some or all of the discount he received. This applies to most sales, assignments and sub-lettings for a period of more than twenty-one years. But a disposal to a spouse or resident members of the family who have lived with the tenant for a year or more is exempt from these provisions, and so are disposals by will, or on a divorce following a court order, or disposals to someone who could have bought (or does buy) compulsorily, or disposals of part of the property not including the residential part.

The amount to be repaid depends on when the sale, assignment or sub-letting takes place, as follows:

sale made	*discount repayable*
in the first year	100%
in the second year	80%
in the third year	60%
in the fourth year	40%
in the fifth year	20%

So, if Mr Samuel Taylor had tried to make a quick profit by selling his house in the second year after he had bought it, he would have been liable to repay £6,400.

The obligation to repay takes effect as if the landlord had a legal mortgage over the property for the amount of the discount. This 'mortgage' ranks in priority after the council mortgage or any charge securing money borrowed by the tenant from the Housing Corporation, any building society, bank or insurance company to finance the right to buy. A landlord should immediately protect his charge (against a sale by the tenant within the five year period) by registering a caution or notice at the Land Registry.

(*Note*: When the provisions of the Housing and Planning Act 1986 are brought into effect, the five-year period will be reduced to three years, and the five 20%-steps will become three steps of one-third of the discount. Many of the provisions of the Act will not come into effect until regulations have been drawn up and implemented.)

In some cases, a secure tenant does not have an unrestricted right to sell after 5 years. In certain rural areas, in particular areas of outstanding natural beauty and National Parks, there are restrictions on the persons to whom a secure tenant who has bought his home may sell it – for example, only to someone who lives or works in the area. In these areas, the possibility of such a restriction is

choosing the time for buying and selling

It is not necessarily in the best interests of the tenant to serve a notice of intention to exercise his rights to buy at the earliest opportunity, because for every extra year he waits he will get an extra 1% discount. For example, on a house valued at £50,000 this means an extra £500 discount every year.

A tenant should therefore be aware of the precise date on which his qualifying occupation began, because it could be a matter of only days, whether or not he gets an extra 1% discount.

Against this have to be weighed two factors: first, the valuation is on the date the tenant serves his notice of intention to buy, and property prices usually rise by more than 1% a year. So, while it may be worth an intending tenant waiting just a few days, it may not be worthwhile for say, something approaching a year. Second, the longer a tenant waits to exercise his right to buy, the later will be the date when the discount he has to repay to the landlord on any future sale is reduced.

As for selling, the tenant should, within the first three years, consider carefully whether he should wait until the expiration of a further year before selling. Every time a year expires since the date of the purchase, the owner would have to repay one-third less to the landlord on any sale.

the procedure

STEP I

The tenant serves *Notice Claiming the Right to Buy* on his landlord (form RTB1). The landlord has to supply form RTB1 within 7 days of receiving a request for it.

Form RTB1 comprises seven sections asking for details of the property, the tenant and members of the tenant's family who wish to share the right to buy; the periods of occupation which will count towards calculating the discount; any previous purchase at a discount from one of the public sector landlords; particulars of any improvements made to the property. The seventh section is for signatures, where all the intending purchasers have to sign.

Form RTB1 also explains what will happen next.

STEP II

Within 4 weeks of receiving form RTB1, the landlord must serve *Notice in Reply to Tenant's Right to Buy Claim* (form RTB2). The period is 8 weeks if the two-year qualifying period includes a period as the tenant of a different landlord.

On form RTB2, the landlord inserts the names of those secure tenants whose claim to buy he admits, and of those whose claim he denies, with the reasons for denying the claim.

If a landlord denies the tenant's claim, the tenant should go to a citizens' advice bureau or legal aid centre and seek legal advice. If his efforts are unsuccessful, he can still go to the county court to try and establish his rights.

STEP III

If the landlord admits the tenant's claim or the tenant successfully establishes his right, the landlord must send the tenant a notice stating the proposed terms of sale. The notice must be served by the landlord within 8 weeks of the service of form RTB2 (in the case of a freehold purchase) or 12 weeks (in cases where a lease is being granted). The notice must state:

○ the price, and how it was calculated
○ tenant's improvements which have been disregarded
○ the discount entitlement, and how this was calculated
○ provisions to be included in the conveyance or lease; if the landlord is to grant a lease and there will be a service charge, an estimate of that charge
○ an explanation of the tenant's right to have the value of the property determined or redetermined by the district valuer
○ details of the tenant's right to mortgage (an application form must be included)
○ details of the shared ownership lease scheme
○ details of the notice to complete procedure.

no delays

The landlord has to deal with the completion of the conveyance or grant of the lease as quickly as circumstances allow. Naturally, the tenant's mortgage arrangements must be finalised and the terms of the lease agreed but, after that, if the landlord unreasonably delays, the tenant can ask the Secretary of State to exercise his default powers to push through the conveyance or grant of a lease.

Where a secure tenant claims a mortgage and this is not enough to meet all the costs of his purchase, he may be able to defer completion of the sale. The tenant should serve on the landlord notice of his wish to defer completion until he can find the extra money to meet all his costs, within 3 months of receiving his mortgage offer; a longer period may be allowed where reasonable. He must also pay a deposit of £100. The deposit is returnable if the sale does not go ahead: if the sale does go through, the deposit will count towards the purchase price. The maximum time for which completion can be delayed is 2 years from the date of service of the form RTB1. A tenant who has the right to defer completion may also be entitled to claim a shared ownership lease.

the first notice to complete
If the tenant delays completing after certain time limits have elapsed, the landlord can serve the tenant with a notice (the 'first notice to complete') requiring him to state whether the delay is due to outstanding matters in respect of a mortgage or the grant of a lease. The tenant is given a reasonable time (at least 56 days) in which to reply. The landlord's notice also states what will happen to the tenant's claim if he fails to comply with a notice to complete, should the landlord subsequently serve one.

No notice requiring an explanation for delay can be served:

○ where the value of the dwelling remains to be finally determined (an example would be where the tenant has asked for a determination by the district valuer)
○ if the tenant has not claimed a mortgage from the local authority, unless nine months have passed since he first could have claimed the mortgage
○ during any period in which the tenant has exercised his right to defer completion
○ while the tenant is claiming a shared-ownership lease.

the second notice to complete
If the landlord gets no reasonable explanation for the delay, he may serve a notice ('the second') on the tenant to complete within the period stated in the notice. This must be a reasonable period, with a minimum of 56 days, and the period can be extended by the landlord. If the tenant does not complete within the stated time, he is treated as having withdrawn his claim to buy his home.

A second notice to complete cannot be served on a tenant who claims a shared ownership lease.

withdrawing a claim

A secure tenant may withdraw his claim at any time by giving written notice (forms are available from law stationers) to his landlord. Theoretically, he may withdraw his claim one day and put in a new claim the next.

cost to the tenant

The tenant usually has to meet the following expenses in addition to the purchase price:

○ His own costs of employing a surveyor and/or solicitor. A tenant is not liable for any legal or other professional fees incurred by the landlord, other than a maximum of £200 in connection with a mortgage provided by the landlord. If his mortgage is from some independent source, he will have to pay the legal costs in connection with it.

○ Stamp duty at the rate of 1% of the price paid where the purchase price is more than £30,000.

○ Land Registry fees, because a tenant who buys his home under the Housing Act has to register his title with the appropriate District Land Registry. The fee depends on the value of the property. There is a simplified Land Registry procedure for right to buy sales.

the right to a mortgage

A secure tenant who has the right to buy, has the right to obtain a mortgage to finance the purchase, usually from his landlord. However, where the tenant's landlord is a housing association, the mortgage is provided by the Housing Corporation.

Where two or more tenants have the right to buy, a mortgage can be obtained jointly by all of them. By pooling their income, they may be able to get a larger mortgage than a sole secure tenant.

The tenant and landlord may agree on the terms of a mortgage (although there is a limit on the amount that can be borrowed). Where there is no such agreement, the following terms will apply.

how much can be borrowed

The amount can exceed what a buyer would normally be able to get on an ordinary mortgage loan: the mortgage can be for more than 100% of the purchase price, but the amount of the mortgage cannot be more than the aggregate of the purchase price plus such of the landlord's costs as are chargeable to the tenant and any costs incurred by the tenant and defrayed by the landlord.

The amount that the tenant may borrow will be reduced if the tenant's available annual income (or, in the case of a joint application, the aggregate income) is insufficient. Regulations have set out the way in which the relevant income is to be established.

The applicant's annual income from all sources must first be calculated, minus, where applicable, an amount equal to any payments made under a maintenance agreement, court order or credit agreement, provided these payments are likely to continue for the next 18 months or more. Deducting these sums from annual income gives the tenant's 'available annual income'. This is then multiplied by a number which depends on his age at the time he gives notice of wanting to exercise the right to buy. The appropriate multiplier is

age on giving notice	multiplier
under 60	2.5
60–64	2.0
65 and over	1.0

So – if Mr Marks (who is under 60) has an annual income of £11,200 and pays £100 per month HP for a car, his mortgage entitlement would be:

	£
annual income	11,200
less annual credit payments	1,200
available annual income	10,000

mortgage advance = £10,000 × 2.5 = £25,000

the term

The conditions of the mortgage repayment may be agreed between the landlord and tenant; in the absence of agreement, the term of the mortgage over which the secure tenant should repay is 25 years, but he may opt for a shorter term or the landlord may extend it. If the tenant buys a leasehold interest of less than 25 years, the mortgage term will be the same as the period of the lease.

interest rate

The Housing Act specifies the rate of interest chargeable where a secure tenant buys from a local authority. The rate is the higher of the standard national rate as declared by the Secretary of State, or the applicable local average rate (broadly speaking $\frac{1}{4}$% above the rate paid by the local authority to borrow the money to provide to a secure tenant).

A secure tenant who buys from a landlord other than a local authority should write to the landlord or the Housing Corporation for an estimate of the initial interest rate.

The interest rate may vary during the mortgage term regardless of who the landlord is.

how to apply for a mortgage under the Act

A secure tenant buying from a housing association claims a mortgage by serving notice in the prescribed form on the Housing Corporation (149 Tottenham Court Road, London W1P 0BN). All other secure tenants serve notice claiming a mortgage on their landlords.

The prescribed form is *Notice Claiming The Right to a Mortgage* (form No 4). It must be sent to a tenant by his landlord along with the notice of terms of sale.

Form 4 asks for details of a secure tenant's income, commitments to be deducted in calculating available annual income.

The form must be served on the landlord (or Housing Corporation if appropriate) within 3 months of receiving the landlord's notice of terms of sale or the determination of the value of the house by the district valuer where the value is disputed. The period may be extended if there are reasonable grounds for so doing.

A landlord or the Housing Corporation must reply to a tenant's claim on form 4 'as soon as practicable'. The reply must state:

○ the amount which in the opinion of the landlord or the Housing Corporation the tenant is entitled to have advanced;
○ the method used to calculate the amount;
○ the provisions which the landlord or the Housing Corporation feels should be included in the mortgage deed.

A statement must accompany the landlord's (or Housing Corporation's) reply, informing the tenant of his rights to defer completion or take a shared ownership lease if the tenant's income does not qualify him for a full 100% mortgage.

other sources of finance
Nothing precludes a secure tenant from seeking a mortgage from sources other than his landlord (or the Housing Corporation) to finance his right to buy, but the tenant has no automatic right to a mortgage from building societies, banks, insurance companies and so on. The availability of a mortgage from the landlord may be particularly important to an older tenant, say above 50 years, because many other lenders may not be prepared to lend to a person of that age.

shared ownership leases
In certain circumstances, a secure tenant may have the right to be granted a 'shared ownership lease'. The idea of the scheme is that, where the tenant cannot afford to buy his home outright, he can instead buy a slice of a long lease; he then has the right to go on purchasing further slices of the long lease until eventually he owns it outright. At that point he can acquire the freehold, provided that the dwelling in question is a house and the landlord owns the freehold interest. In the mean time, the rent that the tenant has to pay to the landlord is reduced according to the size of the slice of the shared ownership lease he has so far purchased.

The right to a shared ownership lease arises where:

○ the tenant's right to buy has been established and his notice claiming to exercise it remains in force
○ the tenant has claimed the right to a mortgage but he is not entitled to a 100% advance (because of his own financial status)
○ the tenant is entitled to defer completion (this means that he must pay a £100 deposit).

The Housing Act sets out the procedure to be followed when claiming a shared ownership lease. It is begun by the tenant serving a notice on the landlord; the landlord must reply within four weeks, either admitting the tenant's claim or rejecting it with reasons. Once the right to the shared lease is established, the Act contains further

provisions dealing with the mechanics of completing the transaction.

tenant's initial share
In the first place, the tenant must purchase at least a 50% share in
the lease. If he prefers, he may purchase a larger share, which must
be a multiple of 12.5%. Therefore, he may begin with 50% or 62.5%
or 75% or 87.5%. He subsequently purchases further 12.5% shares
until he reaches 100%.

tenant's initial contribution and effective discount
The Housing Act contains formulae for working out the price to be
paid for the tenant's initial purchase and for calculating the discount
to which he is entitled.

The initial contribution is determined by the formula:

$$C = S\frac{(V - D)}{100}$$

The effective discount is determined by the formula:

$$E = \frac{S \times D}{100}$$

where C = the tenant's initial contribution
      E = the effective discount
      S = the tenant's initial share expressed as a percentage
      V = the value of the dwelling-house at the relevant time
      D = the discount to which the tenant would be entitled if he
          were exercising the right to buy.

example
Henry lives in a council house valued at £30,000 and has been there
for three years, so that his discount entitlement in right to buy
circumstances is 33%. He now buys a 50% initial share.

$$\text{initial contribution} = \frac{50(30{,}000 - 10{,}000)}{100} = £10{,}000$$

$$\text{effective discount} = \frac{50 \times 10{,}000}{100} = £5{,}000$$

There are further provisions dealing with the calculation of the rent payable by the tenant under a shared ownership lease, and the price to be paid when purchasing further slices of the lease.

A tenant claiming a shared ownership lease is entitled to a mortgage to finance the purchase, according to the rules already explained. If eventually he acquires the whole lease, the £100 deposit counts towards the purchase price.

A tenant who acquires a shared ownership lease cannot exercise the right to buy the freehold under the Leasehold Reform Act 1967 for so long as the annual rent is more than £10.

defective housing

The Housing Act 1985 provides that in certain circumstances assistance may be given to people who purchase their home from a public sector authority where the property in question suffers from a serious defect. The assistance may be financial, but in some cases the authority can be made to repurchase the property.

Assistance is only available in respect of properties which have been designated by the Secretary of State. The Act is intended to apply to system-built houses which suffer from a design fault and whose value is therefore substantially reduced. Only properties which are defective by reason of their design or construction and whose value is substantially reduced as a result, can be designated. When making an order designating a particular type of building, the Secretary of State is required to describe the relevant defect or defects, to name a cut-off date, and to specify a period within which people may make a claim.

An order was made in 1984 naming 22 types of buildings as designated properties for the purposes of the Act. All the properties described are prefabricated concrete homes; the cut-off date is 26 April 1984 (except for so-called Airey Houses, for which it is 8 September 1982). Assistance in respect of all the designated properties must be sought before 1 December 1994.

eligibility for assistance

Only individuals (not companies) are eligible for assistance. The person must own the freehold or a long tenancy (normally this means 21 years or more). The freehold or long tenancy must have been acquired from a public sector authority *either*:

○ before the cut-off date; there must not have been a subsequent sale of the property, *or*

○ within the 12 months following the cut-off date; in this case the purchaser must have been unaware of the defect affecting the property when he purchased it, and the property must have been valued without taking the defect into account. Again there must not have been a subsequent sale of the property, only the original purchaser from the public authority is eligible.

Assistance is not available if the property is let to someone who is a protected tenant under the Rent (Agriculture) Act 1976. Nor may assistance be claimed where the local housing authority are of the opinion that work to the property has been carried out to deal with the defect and that no further work is therefore needed.

procedure

Application for assistance must be made in writing. An application will not be considered from someone who is also making a claim for an improvement grant, an intermediate grant, a special grant or a repairs grant under Part xv of the Housing Act and that claim relates in whole or part to the same defect.

The local housing authority must deal with the application as quickly as is reasonably practicable. If it decides that the applicant is not eligible for assistance, it must give reasons for its decision. If the applicant is eligible, the authority must let him know whether he is entitled to a reinstatement grant or to have the home repurchased by the authority.

reinstatement grants

The usual remedy is for the applicant to receive a reinstatement grant. Such a grant is available where:

○ the property is a house
○ the property would, if the reinstatement work were carried out, be likely to provide satisfactory housing accommodation for at least 30 years and to be suitable security to a mortgagee
○ giving assistance is justified, having regard to the new owner's expenditure likely to be involved on the one hand and the increase in the value of the house on the other
○ reinstatement is not more expensive than repurchase.

There are detailed rules as to procedure, conditions of payment, calculation of the amount to be paid, method of payment and repayment – for example, where the works are never completed. It is up to the new owner to put in hand, commission, supervise etc the carrying out of the work; the housing authority does not take over to get it done.

repurchase
Where the conditions for reinstatement are not fulfilled, or the authority is satisfied that it would not be reasonable to expect the applicant to arrange or await the carrying out of the work required to reinstate the dwelling, the applicant may ask the authority to repurchase the property. The price payable by the authority is 95% of the value of the dwelling at the time that the authority serves a notice on the owner, setting out the proposed terms of acquisition. For these purposes, the value is assessed without regard to the defect which affects the property. A procedure is laid down for determining the value of the dwelling. If necessary, the district valuer will become involved.

Following the repurchase, the authority will normally grant a secure tenancy of the property to the applicant, provided that this has been requested in writing by him. If however this is not possible, for example because the property is unfit to live in or the authority intends to demolish it, an alternative dwelling must be provided.

glossary

abstract
a summary of the proof of a person's ownership of land prepared from the title deeds and other documents

act of parliament
a law made by parliament; a statute

action
process by which one person seeks the help of the civil court to enforce a right against another

agent
person who has authority to act on behalf of another

assignment
sale or transfer of the whole of a tenant's interest in a lease to another person

common law
the traditional law of England and Wales, derived from custom and judges' interpretation (as against statute law)

completion
the final stage of the legal transaction when buying or selling a freehold or leasehold

contract
a legally binding agreement; can be oral, but where it concerns land it should be evidenced in writing

controlled rent
rent in which the maximum level is limited by law

covenant
a promise between landlord and tenant whereby they are bound to do certain things, such as to pay the rent or to repair; may be express or implied

county court
court which deals with small civil cases, including landlord's and tenant's (generally, the amount at stake must not be more than £5,000)

criminal law
the part of the law which punishes behaviour harmful to the community as a whole, as against the civil law which confers rights and duties on individual people

curtilage
piece of ground (such as a courtyard) or part of a building near to and belonging to a house

deed
a document which is 'signed, sealed and delivered'; the seal need not be wax but can be a small round paper disc; delivery is physically handing over with the intention of making it operative (the transfer of the legal title to leasehold property has to be by deed)

demised premises
property which is the subject matter of a lease with certain implied covenants, such as promising that the tenant shall have quiet enjoyment of the premises

determination
when an interest in land comes to an end or ceases

disposition
any transferring of an interest in land, for example a sale, a gift, a lease, or by will

enfranchisement
tenant with long lease buying the freehold of the property under the Leasehold Reform Act 1967

engross
formally to prepare an agreed draft document for execution

equitable interest
rights in a property which fall short of legal title, for example where a lease is not properly created it may be an equitable lease

estate
person's interest in land (may be freehold or leasehold)

execute
to sign, seal and deliver a document

exclusive possession
the right to keep all others out of premises, including the landlord

forfeiture
the means by which a landlord can bring a lease to an early end following a breach of covenant by the tenant

freehold
absolute ownership of real property, which will continue with no limitation of time (as against leasehold)

frustration
a contractual doctrine which relieves the parties from their liabilities under a contract if its performance becomes impossible due to the fault of neither party; frustration may apply to leases (for example, it is possible in some circumstances that a lease may be frustrated by fire)

grant
formal giving or transferring

ground rent
small sum payable periodically to the landlord (the ground owner) by tenant who holds leasehold property on a long lease

high court
the principal court which deals with civil cases in England and Wales; there is no restriction as to the amount at stake

incumbrance
any adverse interest, usually financial such as a mortgage or an undischarged debt, or a restrictive covenant limiting the use to which land may be put

interest in land
a right to, stake in, or any form of ownership of, property such as a house or flat

joint tenants
two (or more) people who hold property jointly in such a way that when one dies the whole property automatically passes to the survivor; under the 1980 Housing Act, two or more people entitled to the right to buy

landlord
the owner of property who grants a lease or sub-lease of the property

land registry
a government department where details of properties with a registered title are recorded

lease
written contract of letting; if for more than 3 years, it must be by deed to be legal

leasehold
ownership of property for a number of years, fixed or periodic, with a lease which sets out the rights and duties of the leaseholder and the landlord (as against freehold)

legal charge
mortgage

licence
the right to use premises, as a personal privilege, without acquiring an interest in the property

offence
a breach of the criminal law

originating application
in certain cases, where there is need for speed, the document which is lodged at the court to start an action

periodic tenancy
a tenancy for a short but definite period (for example, one month) which continues for such further periods until ended by notice

possession action
exercising the powers or controls of ownership; procedure whereby a landlord goes to the court to evict a tenant or other lawful residential occupier

real property
land and any buildings on it

re-entry
retaking possession of a property

registered land
when the title or ownership of freehold or leasehold property has been registered at the Land Registry and its ownership is guaranteed by the state

relief
redress, remedial action, sanctioned by law; for example where the tenant's lease is allowed by the court to continue despite the fact that the landlord has obtained a judgment for forfeiture

residential occupier
someone who lives in the property as his home

reversion
an interest in property which will eventually return to the original owner (or his successors) when the time during which another person holds the property comes to an end

section
a subdivision of a statute, always numbered and in many cases divided into sub-sections

secure tenant
an individual who occupies as his only or principal home a property of which the landlord is a local authority, or a county council, or a housing association or one of a few other public sector landlords

security of tenure
the right to remain in possession

service tenancy
an agreement under which an employee occupies residential accommodation for the better performance of his job

sitting tenant
popular expression for statutory tenant whose lease has expired but who is allowed by law to go on occupying the premises

statute
an act of parliament

statute law
body of law enacted in acts of parliament and their subordinate legislation (as against common law)

statutory instrument
document which makes or confirms legislation that is subordinate to an act of parliament, such as rules, regulations, orders

sub-lease
a lease carved out of another lease, necessarily for a shorter period, created by a person who has only a leasehold interest in the property

sub-tenant
tenant who leases property from a landlord who owns a leasehold, not a freehold interest in that property. It is possible for a chain of tenancies to be built up running from the freeholder (the head-landlord) to his tenant and down to a sub-tenant, then to a sub-sub-tenant and so on. Each tenant becomes the landlord of his own sub-tenant down to the last link in the chain – the tenant in actual occupation

superior landlord
someone with a higher interest than the tenant's immediate landlord; if Mr A, a freeholder, grants a 99 year lease to Mrs B, and Mrs B then grants a 21 year lease to Mr C, Mr A is the superior landlord

tenant
the person to whom a lease is granted

title deeds
documents going back over 15 years or longer which prove the ownership of unregistered property

transfer
a formal deed which passes the freehold ownership of registered land from the seller to the buyer; where the land is unregistered, there is a conveyance (not a transfer)

unregistered land
property – freehold or leasehold – the title or ownership of which has not been registered at the Land Registry, so that the buyer must investigate the validity of the seller's title to it.

Information and help

Anyone in difficulties over renting or letting, or housing rights generally, can go for advice to a **citizens advice bureau**. CAB offices have leaflets and information about local sources of help and services. The address of a local citizens advice bureau can be found in the telephone directory.

SHAC
London Housing Aid Centre
189a Old Brompton Road
London SW5 0AR   (telephone: 01-373 7841 and 01-373 7276)

gives confidential advice and information by telephone or letter (not personal callers) to tenants in London who have a housing problem; can advise on what to do if you are homeless, living in bad conditions, threatened with eviction or looking for accommodation. Publications include:

Private tenants: protection from eviction   70p
Homeless? Know your rights   60p
Rights to repairs, a guide for council tenants   £1.95
Rights to repair: a guide for private and housing association tenants   £1.95

Organisation for Private Tenants
Brixton Enterprise Centre
Bon Marche Building
444 Brixton Road
London SW9 8EJ   (telephone: 01-274 2977)

helps private tenants to form tenants', residents' and leaseholders' associations; publishes a regular newsletter and holds regular meetings for its members; advises tenants, leaseholders, local authorities and other bodies, both voluntary and statutory, about the law as it relates to the private rented sector.

OFPT co-publishes and distributes SHAC publications such as the *Leaseholders' Rights Guide* and a six-pack *Private tenants' rights* which contains separate leaflets on:

Staying put – protection from eviction
Help with rent and rates
Rent payments and fair rents
Your rights to repairs
Harassment and illegal eviction
Getting organised – tenants' associations
Where to go for advice and help.

The membership fee (which is one share in the organisation) is £1.

Shelter
National Campaign for the Homeless
157 Waterloo Road
London SE1 8XF   (telephone: 01-633 9377)
is a national organisation, with a network of groups and members, campaigning on behalf of the homeless and badly housed.

Law Centres Federation
Duchess House
18/19 Warren Street
London W1P 5DB   (telephone: 01-387 8570)
can give you details of your nearest law centre if you need legal advice.

The Department of the Environment and the Welsh Office publish a series of (free) housing booklets, available from rent officers, council offices, citizens advice bureaux and housing aid centres. They include:

Assured Tenancies
  A guide for landlords and tenants

Leasehold Reform
  A guide for leaseholders and landlords

Letting Rooms in your Home
  A guide for resident landlords and their tenants

Letting your Home or Retirement Home
  A guide for home-owners and servicemen who want to let their homes temporarily

Notice to Quit
  A brief guide for landlords and tenants

Regulated Tenancies
  Fair rents and security of tenure explained

Service Charges in Flats
  A guide for landlords and tenants

Shared Ownership
  How to become a home-owner in stages

Shorthold Tenancies
  A guide for private landlords and tenants

The Rent Acts and You
  A brief guide for landlords and tenants

index

CONSUMER PUBLICATIONS

Which? way to buy, sell and move house

takes you through all the stages of moving to another home – considering the pros and cons of different places, house hunting, viewing, having a survey, making an offer, getting a mortgage, completing the purchase, selling the present home. It explains the legal procedures and the likely costs. Buying and selling at an auction and in Scotland are specifically dealt with. The practical arrangements for the move and for any repairs or improvements to the new house are described. Advice is given for easing the tasks of sorting, packing and moving possessions, people and pets, with a removal firm or by doing it yourself, and for making the day of the move go smoothly.

The legal side of buying a house

covers the procedure for buying an owner-occupied house with a registered title in England or Wales (not Scotland) and describes the part played by the solicitors and building society, the estate agent, surveyor, Land Registry, insurance company and local authority. It takes the reader step by step through a typical house purchase so that, in many cases, he can do his own conveyancing without a solicitor; it also deals with the legal side of selling.

Taking your own case to court or tribunal

is for people who do not have a solicitor to represent them in a county court or magistrates' court or before a tribunal. This book tells you the procedures to follow in preparing and presenting your case, what happens at the hearing, what steps can be taken to enforce a judgment, how to appeal if the judgment goes against you. It explains in layman's terms how to conduct proceedings yourself in the county court (arbitration for 'small claims' and open court hearings), in the High Court (rarely appropriate for a litigant-in-person), in a magistrates' court (for both civil and criminal matters), at a social security appeal tribunal (challenging a DHSS benefits decision) and before an industrial tribunal (dismissal cases).

Children, parents and the law
describes the legal responsibilities and rights of a parent, and of a child towards parents, so far as they exist. It deals with illegitimacy, when things go wrong in the family, with education, if a child comes up against the law, when a child has to go into the care of the local authority, and explains what is involved in custodianship, guardianship, adoption, fostering. It sets out at what ages a child can carry out specific activities – from buying a pet to getting married. There is a section explaining the effects of a child being injured and of the death of one or both parents.

Earning money at home
explains how to brush up a skill or hobby into a money-making venture. It gives advice on organising your family and domestic life, on advertising your activities, costing and selling your work, dealing with customers. There is information on statutory and financial requirements for insurance, tax, accounts, VAT, employing others. The book suggests ways in which your experience from a previous job could be utilised, or a skill or hobby developed to a professional standard, or how unexploited energy and ability can be used profitably. Suggestions are made for improving your skills to a higher standard, and the names and addresses are given of organisations that might be helpful.

Starting your own business
for people who have the courage, imagination and stamina to try a new venture on their own, this is a competent guide to help them through the essential steps. It advises on defining precisely what product or skill you have to offer, how to raise the necessary capital and cope with legal requirements. It deals with all the financial aspects: pricing the product, calculating overheads and cash flow, keeping accounts and other records, dealing with taxes including VAT, marketing and selling, premises and insurance. Throughout, sources of advice and information are given to help the small businessman make a success of going it alone.

Approaching retirement
deals with the financial and practical questions that are likely to face you at and before retirement, and helps you plan in advance. The topics covered in detail include pensions (both state and occupational or personal), how to invest a lump sum, the effects of tax, and budgeting generally. Where to live, fitness and health, voluntary work, finding new ways of spending your leisure are among the practical aspects discussed in the book.

some other CA publications
Divorce: legal procedures and financial facts
Living with stress
Understanding allergies
Understanding cancer
Understanding mental health
What to do when someone dies
Wills and probate
The Which? book of insurance
Which? way to repair and restore furniture

Consumer Publications are available from Consumers' Association, Castlemead, Gascoyne Way, Hertford SG14 1LH and from booksellers.